The Story and Confessions of My Life: What Is My Life?

Book I

by

Rev. Dale John Arnold

DORRANCE
PUBLISHING CO
EST. 1920
PITTSBURGH, PENNSYLVANIA 15238

Dorrance Publishing Co
585 Alpha Drive
Pittsburgh, PA 15238
Visit our website at *www.dorrancebookstore.com*

ISBN: 978-1-6386-7136-7
eISBN: 978-1-6386-7671-3

Contents

This book is dedicated to Jesus.

Conceptionhood

I had to make up this word. I have something against the abortionists: They kept this word out of the dictionary! On second thought, they allowed me to wordsmith it! Noah Webster must have been an abortionist. He kept *conceptionhood* out of the dictionary, but he added the word *abortion*. Can you believe it? According to the Merriam-Webster online dictionary, the word *abortion* has been in existence in the English language since the sixteenth century.[1] That is approximately five hundred years difference from today's date. Isn't it time that *conceptionhood* be written in the dictionary? *Conceptionhood* must be on its path into wordhood!

For conservatives, according to our mindset, our lives started out at conception; we became human beings before liberals. Liberals, on the whole, are younger than their conservative cousins, if they are called family, because of their belief system. The lives of their children did not start until birth. It has been recorded at the County Clerk's office at birth or thereafter, but conception was only recorded in the mind of those who knew conception occurred. God knew at what time; man guesses, though. My individual life entered into the stage I have just named *conceptionhood*. Though not all of society may have agreed that I was a human being at that moment. For that reason, the newly wordsmithed word *conceptionhood* was invented just today, April 30th, 2020, at 1:30 p.m. EST, for the purpose of indoctrinating an abortionist liberal America that *conceptionhood* is a part of lifelike babyhood, toddlerhood, childhood, girlhood, boyhood, ladyhood, personhood, peoplehood, humanhood, or aunthood.[2] It is not only becoming someone in a stage of life, but it is the first part of life itself when a flash of light sparkles forth!

---

[1] Merriam-Webster. "Abortion." *Merriam-Webster.com*. March 10, 2021. http://www.merriam-webster.com/dictionary/abortion.
[2] Farlex. "Words containing hood." The Free Dictionary. Accessed March 10, 2021. http://www.thefreedictionary.com/words-containing-hood.

In America, our birthdays are considered that which makes our age. *Conceptionhood* is not considered part of our age. Those of us religious enough to believe that life starts at conception have told lies, then. We have lied about our age since our beliefs are that our age starts at conception. The religious right gets very upset about abortion, confessing it as murder, but they still ignore adding the time in the womb of the mother to their age. Isn't that murder, too? Or, it is, shall we say, confessing one thing: the baby did not exist from conceptionhood to birth, writing it again and again the same birthdate without acknowledging the time of conceptionhood till birth; yet, at the same time, screaming bloody murder at those who go to abortion clinics for committing murder of a child.

No one really knows their real age from the date of their conception. In fact, if we had to truly say the right date of our age, which included our conception, all would have trouble remembering their age. Each of us would be confounded. Conservative America, nonetheless, could say their age from conception, if possible; liberals would only stick to birthdates. Every time someone states their age, though, they are not factually telling us the truth, in my opinion: only those who believe that life starts at birth or their conception was possibly from January to March.

Conceptionhood in the womb began I
Knowing not the date
Knowing not my name
Mother neither knowing either
Life initiated unknowingly
Conception sparks a mystery
And a debate to who I am

Could you imagine that question? "When were you conceived?" One day, mothers may have the technology at home for a flash of light to sparkle in front of them, recorded by Alexa, making the announcement conception has begun!

ALEXA: JOE AND TAMILA: YOU ARE NOW DAD AND MOM! IT'S TIME TO CELEBRATE CONCEPTIONHOOD! IN THE MORNING, DON'T FORGET TO GO TO THE COUNTY CLERK'S OFFICE AND RECORD THAT WHICH I DISCOVERED FOR YOU!

That alone should cause a celebration to take place for the lucky parents! Or embarrassment that Alexa was watching and in the know! It would really help us get our ages right, too. If scientists and inventors work together to build an invention that creates a sound or light for Mom and Dad to know exact conception dates, we will have solved this mystery. The problem is, scientists are liberals, and inventors are conservatives.

When was I conceived? I can only guess. If I were to approach my mom and dad to question the date, first, they would have no idea. Secondly, it would cause much embarrassment for both sides. Perhaps that is why they settled on birthdates instead of conception dates?

One probable date of conception for me could be November 13th, 1965. I prefer the sound of August 13th, 1966. November of 1965 just sounds too old.

To give you my age, according to my religious beliefs, I cannot and will not, not only because it is beyond my ability, but also it is because I do not want to lie (Since I started this book and noted this belief in this book as recorded, I have been asked my age countless times, especially online. Research scientists have virtually tried to impede this book as full of lies).

Moreover, in contemplation of the date of conception, it adds instead of subtracts from the number of our age. Most people probably have this idea: the older one gets, the younger they wish to appear to others, especially ladies. This is, without reservation, the true reason why the birthdates were settled on. The dates of our ages appear younger than reality. Everyone is truthfully older than they say. It is almost like reading a fiction book when reading an application of a person's age. I have not made any conclusion as to how I might answer this question morally. Perchance, I must consult my pastor. The ladies will also opt for the younger age.

Questions come rapidly from the left and the right, people, surveys, doctors, job applications, all expecting a customary response. In answering such questions at an appointment as a donor of blood, my age had to be placed on computer record. Could I tell the truth? Shall I not be like everyone that agrees with abortionists that life only starts at birth? Do not fret! Bio Life Plasma Services explained to me that I am not able to give plasma due to the fact that I was in Germany from January of 1986 to May of 1987,[3] and that, in my conclusion of the reasons for my blood rejection was the following: I could spread mad cow disease through my blood or plasma donation. I wondered why I had become an inpatient at, at least, four different mental hospitals: China (2003), South Korea (2005), Russia (2006), and Azerbaijan (2008). I had become mad.

---

[3] Jim Kling. "Mad Cow Disease Restricts Blood Donation." WebMD. February 21, 2003. http://www.webmd.com/men/news/20030221/mad-cow-scare-linked-to-blood-shortage.

Insanehood

I had no idea what had become of me. I ended up in mental hospitals under a heavy dosage of drugs. Forced to take medicine as indicated by the doctor, my mind under drugs or not under drugs was the same: all was a mental blur either way. The medicine gave me no clue as to the reasons of my proposed insanity. I was later to learn I had become insane—Um, that is, I had a mental disorder—but I had no idea as to how I had achieved this. It seems this achievement is not a regular achievement. It is like having an illness of the mind. To professionals keen on not degrading a person's self-worth, they have termed it a mental disorder. For this writing, I will just use more the term insanity. The term *psycho* has become more derogatory than it should be, made by movies to place within the mind of the audience and society the threat of the person who is insane and term it something that brings a bad fame upon the person, coupling it with trying to murder other people.

That is not my goal, though, to get into all of that. My goal here instead is to ask the question, How did it all come about? What made my mind go insane? That is a question that still, in just searching nonchalantly on the web, is a question that bothers professionals that they really cannot pinpoint. That is the main question that really requires an answer. The doctors had not shared any clues as to the reasons for my insanity: they only made it known that I had a mental disorder. According to dictionary.com, the term *insane* is no longer used medically,[4] but other derogatory terms that mark the individual caught in the struggle between reality and fiction is psycho or psychopath.

"How are you today, Mr. Arnold?" said Ralph (the psychiatrist).

---

[4] "Insane." Dictionary.com. Accessed March 11, 2021.
https://www.dictionary.com/browse/insane.

"I'm making up my mind how I feel today."

"Did you have any bad dreams?" asked Ralph.

"Nightmares? Isn't that what you call them?"

"Why, yes. Have you had any of those, or what have you been thinking about?"

"(After about three minutes) I've been thinking why no psychiatrists have asked me any questions while in the psycho wards. They just observe my actions, look at my eyes, and make judgments from there. They are not involved in therapy."

(The above conversation did not take place. It only exemplifies how some psychiatrists chose not to have discussions with the insane. This was not true for all psychiatrists. There was, in fact, one who did, in Azerbaijan).

Insanity is a mystery how it comes about
The mind of the insane when made cure
Contemplates on the episodes of the past
The strange occurrences that come about
At the last stage, it appears
A thought surfaces: Why did I become insane?
Doctors, psychiatrists, psychologists all search
With their clear minds of thought
However, it blurs in discussion
When they question the insane
The insane try making the story clear
With the mix of drugs and an insane mind
And, a clear-headed doctor looking for answers from a psycho
One comprehends why no one has come to any conclusions

Gaining entrée to the discussion with a psycho
To find the trigger of insanehood
Only does one thing: it generates confusion as to the cause
In the mind of the psychiatrist, ready to prescribe more drugs
The option, then, is not to discuss
With the psycho his thoughts

Only careful observation is given
In the case of the person
Who fell ill those days
Wondering what had been going on
To provoke the society to call an ambulance
And forcibly take him to an insane ward

I was hurting not even a bird
But the call was made since my mind
Was off the wall
Not making sense of my conversation
Not making it work as normal
And having trouble with the meaning of the day
The meaning of time as it should
It was more a timeless moment
The mind absorbed in other things
That were not normal
Thus, the professionals were called
They made that dreaded call
The feeling of a call of betrayal
Not caring for one like one should
Instead, that dreaded call was made
To authorities to force one
To remove them from society
Putting them behind four walls
Not letting freedom in their lives
Because their conversation was stranger
Than it ever should have been

Mad cow disease had nothing to do with it, though. This might be a way to blame the insanity that had enveloped me. The doctor at the Biolab gave me a reason to point to: a cow did it. Psychiatrists would probably agree. I cannot and will not agree to it. That reason was only introduced into my mind in the year 2020, seventeen years after my first episode. Does it take that long to come to a reason for insanity?

You may believe a cow did it to make me go insane, but I will not. I am not insane describing the reason for my insanity. I have warmed up to a much better painting of reality of why I had become insane. I think whoever came up with the idea that I would spread mad cow disease was insane at the time of their suggestion. They would be able to point to the fact that I was in the mental hospital time and time again, and that any suggestion on my part could never be true! Therefore, in my defense, I have begun writing this like a thesis to provide proof that mad cow disease had nothing to do with my insanity and that I should have every right to donate blood. I have come to a sincere conclusion as to the proposed reasons for my insanity. Yet I am not in the mood to address this in a sentence now. The picture would only be blurry. There must be a full-fledged drawn-out case for innocent citizens to view the clearer landscape.

Since I now know the reasons for my insanity, anyone hearing my suggestions would probably think I am bananas. Society prefers the doctor's explanation rather than a psycho's thesis. Who would not? The only people who might listen to psychos are psychos themselves, and those who listen to the doctors must be healthy. However, even considering the suggestion that mad cow disease forced me into a lunatic life for some time is but a crazy idea. The psycho himself would not even consider the idea! However, the doctor would! And, since the doctor would, everybody else would, too!

A cow did it. For me, that is the most ridiculous idea I have ever come across in a lab. Notwithstanding, society at large promotes the idea that all doctors that have their licenses are sane and only patients could be insane, especially those who have had mental disorders. Even in a court of law, the defense attorney would probably laugh on the inside because in no way, in society at large, are doctors insane. That just does not happen, and it is just not possible. Their ideas are the best; someone who has become insane is scrapped for rationality. In fact, several offices for job applicants probably throw the applications away for those who have once tasted of insanity. They prefer the clearer picture rather than a blurred one.

Since I do not think I will ever become a doctor, I will always be on the side that could become insane and the side that nobody wishes to believe.

Why? The reason is clear: I had been an inpatient in at least four mental hospitals in the past. Who could possibly believe me? My audience would probably only be inpatients at the mental hospital, then. Well, nonetheless, I must start somewhere.

Here, then, is my thesis...

Excuse me for this rant, but to say, though, that cows had something to do with my insanity is a make-believe cover up! Cows could never, ever have anything to do with my insanity, not even mad cows, nor their beef! The bulls might have but not the cows!

Cows did it, say they
One way to pass the blame
Cows cannot defend themselves
Neither can an insane man
All side with the doctor

Infanthood

I was born August 13th, 1966, in a hospital in Midland, Michigan. That is no lie. Good thing it was not a mental hospital. They would have kept me there. Since I was born at a hospital in Midland, Michigan, it was called my hometown. Because I had no choice in the matter, I cried at birth.

In reality, Midland, Michigan, is a safe town, but I did not know that at birth. If I had known that it was a safe town, I would not have cried. Just ask the local police station in Midland, Michigan, and they will confirm it. In fact, Midland, in 2018, was named one of the safest cities to retire in,[5] but looking at my financial situation, I will probably never retire. And in reading *Essays of Liberty VIII* by The Foundation for Economic Education, Poirot states that in taking someone else's taxes, that is, Social Security, is actually taking away from others the right to their income to enjoy one's own leisure.[6] Though the idea is one has paid in for years to the fund, to Poirot, it still flies in the face of reason for one's own responsibility.

The retirement community, if it knows how many times I had been in a mental hospital, will probably be so glad that I will not be moving in to join them.

On August 21st, 1966, I must have been sprinkled at a Lutheran ceremony and given a godmother. However, I do not remember I had been sprinkled nor do I remember anything about that day or the name of my godmother. Since my mind was so small, I could not record the pictures! That realization that I had been sprinkled and given a godmother did not return to memory until the age of fifty years old. That flashback was one of the slowest in my life's history!

---

[5] "Why Midland," City of Midland, Accessed June 4th, 2022, https://cityofmidlandmi.gov/1828/Why-Midland.

[6] Paul L. Poirot. *Essays on Liberty VIII* (New York: The Foundation for Economic Education, Inc.), 38.

Retirementhood

Retirement, to me, is like enlightenment to the Buddhist: it is just a dream. My inclination is to work the rest of my life. Isn't that what God had told Adam after his sin?

"In the sweat of thy face shalt thou eat bread, till thou return unto the ground; for out of it wast thou taken: for dust thou *art*, and unto dust shalt thou return."[7]

As Christians and as Americans, though, we have gotten around that verse. We have come up with retirement: A way to make a living through the taxes of others. Everyone looks forward to retirement, and many look forward to not working. I mean, there are people who get on welfare so as not to work. There are people who retire early so as not to work. I, however, wish to continue to work up until the day I die, if possible. If I do not die, I will have gone up in the rapture as my means of retirement!

Social Security was signed into law by President Roosevelt August 14th, 1935, of which he stated, "we have tried to frame a law which will give some measure of protection to the average citizen and to his family against the loss of a job and against poverty-ridden old age. "[7]However, included in my short research, I found that before the Great Depression, the elderly were faced with poverty, and Social Security actually alleviated millions of the elderly destined towards poverty. [9]That said, that is an accomplishment. The Social Security tax was actually signed into law by President Roosevelt, but it does not allow

---

[7] Gen. 3:19

[7] "Social Security." *Historical Background and Development of Social Security.* Social Security History. Accessed June 19th, 2021. https://www.ssa.gov/history/briefhistory3.html.

[9] Kathleen Romig. "Social Security Lifts More Americans Above Poverty Than Any Other Program." Center on Budget and Policy Priorities. Accessed March 11, 2021. https://www.cbpp.org/research/social-security/social-security-lifts-more-americans-above-poverty-than-any-other-program

for Americans to use one's own voluntary will to give. Instead, it is, as I have understood, those things introduced by law are, simply put, by force. Anything that the government mandates takes away our liberty to give out of our hearts. It does provide, one could say, for the elderly, but that is by mandate and, again, I say, not by our voluntary will. In China, the trend is living with their aged parents.

This is one belief I wish I could fulfill, though, to never retire. I wish society would allow me to work until I die, getting a paycheck every month, because I intend to never become insane again. Further, I hope my body allows me not to retire but to continue to work until I pass from this life to the next. Do you know how not having enough money each month does to the mind and how it causes stress? Further, there is the pressure of being retired and not having a job, thinking that one has worked all his life, then, suddenly, one stops working and begins living on a funded check on a monthly basis. How does that make a person feel? Our moms and dads have taught us independence, but it returns our lives to dependence. I mean, if I am going to get a paycheck, I think I would prefer having worked for it or have made some type of financial investments that assist my living expenses. Social Security, maybe they say, is a type of investment. Nevertheless, I would say, it is never best to depend upon a system. Rather, one should depend on God to get one through, and doing so through work. Besides, they have stated, the system might just run out of money. What is, though, the elderly to do? I might just have to get in the same boat.

If I get to the point where someone says I must retire, I will probably return to my insanity. I must try my best, though, to keep my sanity. If I don't, they will give reasons to either put me into a mental hospital or a nursing home, and if I do, the nurses who care for me will, no doubt, be the ones who will become insane.

Thus, I have become a writer to fulfill that goal of never retiring. A writer's age has little importance on his acceptance of his books. I have never asked anyone, nor have I ever heard anyone ask a writer's age before they purchased a book. It must be that Barnes and Noble keeps that a secret hidden. Could you imagine society asking the publisher or a seller of books how old the author was at the time of the publishing of his or her book or even his or her age at present?

"Did you find everything all right?" said the bookseller.

"Yes, however, I did not find the age of the author at the time of writing of these two books, *God's Way to Ultimate Health* by Rev. George H. Malkmus, Lit D. and Michael Dye. And this one by Catharina Ingelman-Sundberg called *The Little Old Lady Who Broke All the Rules: A Novel*," responded the book buyer.

"That is a good question! Glad you asked! I'll have to do some research. Just a minute!" After a short research, "Rev. George H. Malkmus, Lit D., must have been fifty-eight years old or so when he had written the book.[8]Michael Dye must also be around that age since he has gray hair. As for Catharina Ingelman-Sundberg, I cannot find her age. I'm not sure why."

"I see her picture."

"Do you still wish to buy these?"

"Since Rev. George H. Malkmus, Lit D. is eighty-three years old and retired, I will not buy his book. But since Catharina Ingelman-Sundberg does not look retirement age, I will go ahead and buy her book."

"Huh?"

This, to me, is how silly it sounds to retire in my opinion. People who are older should be respected in society, but I think many of those at that age do not want to continue work. They prefer to rest from their hard labors of those many years. I am already getting to that point. I really do not have an option one way or the other: I must work.

Finding the check-out counter did he
At the local bookstore you see
The man asked the author's age
The cashier thought a silly question it was
The only reason you see
Was to find if the man was retired
So he would not purchase the book, you see
This is how silly it would really be!

---

[8] Rev. George Malkmus. "God's Way to Ultimate Health: A Common Sense Guide for Eliminating Sickness." NEW BOOK! God's Original Diet – By Rev. George Malkmus. Accessed March 11, 2021. https://www.myhdiet.com/healthnews/rev-malkmus/new-book-gods-original-diet-by-rev-george-malkmus/.

Kindergartenhood

My memory started when I attended kindergarten at Eastlawn Elementary School in Midland, Michigan. (At the writing of this book, Eastlawn Elementary school has been decapitated—it has been torn down! I started this book, and they started tearing the school down! Erasing the evidence was complete!). My memory began because of two good-looking girls in kindergarten: Becky Chamberlain and Sherry Looper. To this day, almost fifty years later, I remember their names so clearly. These names have not been forgotten.

The kindergarteners played four square during recess, too. Every recess, I loved playing four square. It was the kind of game I could win. Yes, I got to the highest rank on the court often. I do not think Sherry Looper and Becky Chamberlin played though. I would probably have lost on purpose.

My dreams also started in kindergarten. The dream was to meet Sherry Looper or Becky Chamberlain outside of class. I remember the announcement: a girl, Sherry Harder, across the park was having a birthday party, and I was invited. She had invited Becky Chamberlain and Sherry Looper too. I could not miss that! As a kindergartener, that was the most important date I can remember. For me, it would have turned out to be the most fascinating day of my entire career as a schoolboy: *a dream come true.* There was no holiday, no other celebration, no other event that put more importance on my school career and a start towards romance than that day! It had become the most important date of my five-year-old life.

As a five-year-old boy, I had the utmost concern to be attending the birthday party, along with the other neighborhood girls. The date on the calendar was selected, fixed, and remembered. I had it all planned out for my five-year-old mind: I was going! My dream required reality! There was a possibility I could wind up having my first girlfriend! That was so important to me, to select or dialogue with the most beautiful girls in the world at that time!

However, that day I was grounded. I know not the reason why I got grounded on the most important day of my life! That has been forgotten. The only thing that sticks to my memory like the strongest superglue in the world is that on the most important day of my kindergarten life, school life, and academic career, I was grounded. Mom gave me a jail sentence. It was just for a day. However, it was the most important day of my life. I had been enslaved! To this day, nothing comes back to my mind as to the reasons of my being grounded, but the only thing that troubled my mind so much on that day was when I looked out the lengthy windows from our family room towards the park, I could see the very pretty damsels playing on the monkey bars, probably waiting for me! However, I was enchained by my mother! That was the most depressing day of my entire career as a kindergartener! How could I face any more kindergarten days? How would I feel about school from then on? From that day forward, I lost my school vision, my education vision, studying vision, and girlfriend vision. It was only stored as a day that I lost the most tremendous opportunity in my career! Thus, at five years of age, I had my first live nightmare in my home. That nightmare has remained in my memory bank even after these almost fifty years. Your first live nightmare does not erase, especially when it concerns being jailed by Mom and losing an opportunity to communicate with the two most beautiful kindergarteners! For me, at that detrimental school age to continue on an upward path, there was a must to be at that party! Everything spiraled downhill, like off a cliff! That day I hit a brick wall—a humungous live nightmare drained the blood out of my heart.

My schoolboy career had ended...
"Yea, though I walk through the valley of the shadow of death.[9]"
Kindergarten was the happiest school year
Meeting a lot of pretty girls
Having joy playing games
The joy rang on with a birthday invitation
The ultimate peak of excitement for the entire year
Drowned out by disappointment
Grounded by Mom for reasons unclear

[9] Ps. 23:4

Third-Grade-Hood

First and second grade were erased from my memory. It took two years to recuperate.

The beginning of the third grade, I began seeing the light again. Memory was intact. However, this time, I was not fascinated by any of the girls—at least I don't recall any good-looking ones. No names of any are in my memory list.

Instead, it was the slim, tall, elegant, and extremely attractive teacher! On the first day of school, by the students' excellent recommendation, the third-grade teacher was selected as my favorite. Watching her teach and taking everything in would be like starting the car engine once again! I could see where I was headed! My school career had a beam of light, ready to move forward!

We were all sitting down at our desks. Pleasantly, my excitement had beamed for two reasons: First, I had a new friend called Brian May.[10] He had black hair, a freckled face, cool black eyes, and a cool look about him. To me, he looked like a cool friend; to others, he wanted to show the fact that no one should mess with him. Second, the first pretty elegant teacher was the best-looking teacher I had ever seen! She attracted all of us, at least, in my mind. She was gorgeous, though I still did not know the word gorgeous. I later added it to my vocabulary list of words.

And my luck was starting to unfold! Brian May had sat right behind me. He was a cool dude who had worn cowboy boots. Cowboy boots were worn by students who wanted to look tough, act cool, and put on a good show so the entire school, that is, no one, absolutely no one should mess with him!

---

[10] In third grade, the name of the student may not have been Brian May; instead, it may have been another student. However, Brian May was possibly the student I had met in seventh grade. Yet, the details about Brian May are the same, except, possibly, for the grade—He still had the boots, the details of the looks, the coolness, and so on. The information concerning the friend sitting behind me was just that—He was a friend, but the details of which are included about Brian May were all Brian's.

Cowboy boots did not measure intelligence. Cowboy boots were the type of apparel that measured a person's coolness. They were made for third graders like Brian May. He scuffed the heels on the floor as he walked. I later learned that was the reason why he was cool. He could walk with his cowboy boots on, scuff them on the floor, and the other students should have thought two things regarding him: He is cool and tough. And everyone must keep their distance unless you are his friend, or you want a fight!

On the first day of third grade, I got into his inner circle of friends. That was what I call cool!

Stepping into that third-grade classroom started my memory again. In fact, it was the first day of school that my memory became so glued to. It has not erased.

Two memorable people entered my life
A newly found friend
And a teacher I gave trust and respect
These two friends, I could see
Would motivate my school career once again
My dream gave birth to sparkles that first day of school
There was much planning to do.

And then...

BAM!!

It was during that class I felt so comfortable, relaxed, and willing to turn around and chat with my new amigo. While the slender, tall, elegant teacher instructed all of us from the front of the classroom, using her blackboard with the skill of an expert, I was busy chatting to Brian May. I felt refreshed, energetic, and ready to start studying to the best of my ability with dreams of an excellent school career in mind once again. My dreams had faded for two years for having gotten grounded on the day I had my dream crushed—of meeting two of the most beautiful kindergarten girls! Now, the dream could sparkle once again! I had felt the emotion driving my inner sense to desire, adore, and love studying in the classroom once again! I could see it in my eyes: the pretty, stalky teacher and a new cool friend! Third grade, I could see it—this would be the unfolding of the red carpet for my desires of school to skyrocket above the highest sky-scraper! This could please Mom and Dad with high scores on the report card!

The dreams were boiling in my mind: study extremely hard—which really would be extremely easy considering the pretty teacher—and keep up a great friendship with Brian May. These two had gotten me the right two ingredients for putting my best efforts into studying. Wow, my dreams had already started! My mind began daydreaming again for success in school! Third grade would see higher grades and more social activities for me. I was on the road to happiness finally! I was seeing red all over the place—after two years of erased drudgery! The heartbreak of that peak moment to meet those two beautiful girls on Sherry Harder's birthday would be easier, much easier to get over, of missing out on the opportunity of a lifetime!

BAM!

Without warning, a palm of a hand slaughtered my desktop (poor desk-top!), a loud crash that drove the point home to every single student within that classroom! I was in shock! I wondered whose large hand had come down on my desktop, palm downward. Dumbfounded, I turned around stunned, frightened, and unnerved. All eyes were upon me, glaring eyes, eyes that were colossal! I was not the only one shocked at such a forceful blow to the desktop, but all eyes and all other conversations at once were stopped! A pin dropping on the floor could make the loudest noise at that moment!

Turning around with a pale face, I looked up with innocent eyes at the tall, glaring, slender, and beautiful angry face of the teacher! My intense conversation with my new friend had abruptly ended, and it had ended for the rest of the entire day and, unbeknownst to me, the rest of the school year, too. It was so shocking to realize from whom this big bang on my desk had come! The charming eyeful of a dazzling and stunning teacher scowled at me with black and dark eyes! Her perpetually smart mouth opened wide to bellow a shriek of hideous rebuke! Her rebuke, I do not recall, because I had already forgiven her of her attitude for squealing at me, but what happened next handed over the second worst live nightmare!

The time frame of my first day of third grade was not analyzed. The memory of time lapse was not functional yet. Since we had the entire day with the new instructress, it may have been thirty minutes or two hours that had passed. I had been busily chatting with Brian May when the instructor approached my desk, slammed her palm on the top of my desk, and demanded I turn around and be silent in her classroom while she was instructing. The rest of the day passed without me uttering a word to my friend. I glued my eyes to the teacher with my lips shut tightly. I was mesmerized.

Nothing was really recalled as to my reaction or even if I resented anything. No resentment surfaced at that time.

Later, though, I had concluded, she must have been jealous of me chatting with Brian.

The day following, a few of us students who had misbehaved in her classroom, the ones who had also received a slammed palm on their desks—I was not the only one—were also selected as students by her or by the school as refuse. The six or so rejected students got in line the following day and were escorted to another classroom headed by an unsightly teacher who failed to smile. The undesirables were disallowed to observe the model instructress from then on and forced to put eyes upon Ms. Unsightliness. We had all flunked the first day. Since we were not given any instructions as to how long this change was in effect, nor did we have any opportunity to apologize for our misbehavior and return, I assumed that it was temporary and that my cohorts and I would be able to return to Ms. Beauty Pageant. Therefore, I was on my best behavior. Nevertheless, even though I desired and wholeheartedly wanted to return and would have given an apology, I had been forcefully removed, feeling I had committed an unpardonable sin, not able nor given opportunity to recuperate from. As day after day passed, the hope for return diminished, and so did the desire to study with motivation. I do not recall learning the rules, but they were laid down that day with this thought: actions speak louder than words.

The other teacher, sadly, was not pretty at all. In fact, in sitting in her classroom, the best thing to do was to look away from her. There is, in my memory, no recount of her teaching anything. I remember nothing at all, except for one assignment. That is the only memory that I have. The rest of the entire year's memory is gone. Even my memory could not keep her in it.

Sadness ensued for having chatted with my friend; repentance, too, not only from the fact that Ms. Beauty Pageant was missed, but my newfound friend was forcefully deposed! Day after day had passed, and no change had been offered. I received no explanation, no possibility of return. I had committed an unpardonable crime in the classroom, and I was never, ever to return. I had become a criminal with a record. Trying to make a friend in class competing for attention was hailed as a crime, and the jail sentence was moving the criminals to Ms. Unsightliness. I was totally upset. This change was not for a week, for a month, or for a few months. It was for the entire year! I had committed a felony. Another live nightmare was experienced in a day and the live nightmare continued with Ms. Unsightliness. I learned right away not to mess with the law!

In summary, on my first day of third-grade class, I had lost a friend and the teacher I liked due to my irreverent behavior. I quickly adjusted to a shy boy. Instead of creating a conversationalist, a person who loved to study, Ms. Beauty Pageant rewarded me with an ugly teacher, a requirement to learn shyness, and learning to stare out the window.

"And that ye study to be quiet, and to do your own business, and to work with your own hands, as we commanded you."[11]

I needed to highlight and memorize the term *strict*. It was my new vocabulary word learned.

Felon was I.

Crime committed: making the teacher jealous. .

To tally up the punishment received from Ms. Beauty Pageant:

1. Humiliation in front of my newly found friend, Brian May, and all of my new classmates.
2. Loud, undesirable noise forced on my desk.
3. Forced to understand rules of action.

---

[11] I Thess. 4:11

4. A disdainful look for not recognizing and honoring the new teacher.

5. No opportunity to apologize with no explanation that I should apologize.

6. A year's worth of class with Ms. Unsightliness.

7. Compounded punishment: failing eyesight due to being forced to study Ms. Unsightliness.

8. Not able to observe Ms. Beauty Pageant.

Length of punishment: The rest of the year.

Lesson learned: beauty is expensive!

In Ms. Unsightliness's class, my memory only allowed me to record one event. This was an event she had requested the students do: The students were to write sentences with certain words. One of the words she had written was either *teacher* or *hate*. I would guess that the word *hate* was the word she requested, but my memory has failed to give valid confirmation. Nevertheless, if that was the indicated word, she was asking for trouble.

Of all the sentences, also, that I had written one day, which, I suppose, were five, only one stands recorded, even to this day. I had taken this word and used it appropriately with all the grammatical correctness that should have been in a sentence. The sentence itself had no grammatical errors. It was fine-tuned to its correctness. I could not have been prouder of myself coming up with this sentence. I am not sure if conscience sounded an alarm or not. I do not believe so. I had written it with the innocence of any child of any English classroom. I had simply written four words, nothing more, nothing less. The sentence was the following:

"I *hate* my teacher."

I turned the paper in to her, thinking nothing of anything that might transpire afterwards. In truth, I do not recall anyone explaining to me about my first amendment rights. I assume that in third grade, as I was, that subject had not been broached upon yet. And I do not believe my family had mentioned it in conversation to us kids, either. Therefore, without realizing that my liberty was guaranteed under the US Constitution, I had written this sentence as to a feeling that any student could have towards their teacher. It was just the fact that the word *I* caught the teacher's attention. Since I was attending a public school in the heart of America, I had every right to free speech. Well, maybe I was taking two liberties at the same time: the right to free speech and freedom of the press. Though it was not something I shared with the class at all. I had not engaged with speaking with anyone about it. My memory does not allow me any other classmates' faces or names within the class at all. The only one that was recorded was Brian May, but he was not in this classroom. Thus, I had people in my class I had not cozied up to nor talked with at all concerning my intentions or bringing bad fame upon the teacher. That was not my intention at all. I did not zero in on that. My intention was purely innocent. I simply used the verb she required within a sentence, formulated it with a few other words, handed it in as though I was doing everything correct. The US Constitution further guaranteed my freedom of the press, even though it was only shared with one other person, and no other person had read it nor knew anything about it at all.

She did read it. I guarantee that.

After the next class, the teacher flagged me down, putting a stop to my exit. I was detained for a minute—um, it was more like twenty minutes—required by the teacher to explain something.

Ms. Unsightliness showed me my paper. She probably pointed directly to my sentence and said the following, "I would like for you to explain to me why you had written this…."

What followed was nothing….I could not answer her. I stood for the entire time silent, not knowing how to respond, for I had nothing against her. In my mind, I was only writing what she had requested. She was then requesting the reasons for writing it. I could not for the life of me figure out why the teacher would ask me this question. Did she not know that she had requested us to write sentences?

But, on second thought…

I have thought about why I had written it. It has taken me forty-five years now, to this date of May 7th, 2020, after all my *psycho* episodes ending up in *psycho wards* in various countries around the globe, to finally figure out why I had written what I had written. I had been born in August 1966 and must have been in the third grade, presumably, eight years from the date of my birth. Thus, since I have now figured out the reason for me writing this sentence, I am now directing this to Ms. Unsightliness. However, if I address her in this fashion, that would not be in a respectful manner. Thus, I shall call her Ms. Teacher for this address.

My sentence was wrong according to the vocabulary word used. It should not have included the word *teacher* singular in it. However, since she was at the brunt of the *attack*, it was the only way that I could have expressed myself. Knowing third-grade vocabulary, I would never have understood how to address the inward feeling. You see, from the experience of being traumatized by Ms. Beauty Pageant (I had easily forgiven her), I could only express it in this way because of what had happened. Thus, it would have correctly stated, *I hate teachers.*

The plural form has made it sound more legit after all these years of analysis. And it was not exactly the fact that the teacher had mistreated me, only in a couple of aspects: since I was a sheep, she had *robbed* me. I have since forgiven the principal of Eastlawn Elementary School, and the fact that I was whisked away from Ms. Beauty Pageant's classroom, and the fact that I had been placed in Ms. Teacher's classroom, that is, Ms. Unsightliness. And at the age of fifty-four, the year 2020, a heartbreaking year nonetheless, I have also forgiven Midland Public Schools for tearing down Eastlawn Elementary School for trying to cover up their mistake made in 1974 of receiving that treatment. They might have even left the paperwork, the historical facts in the rubble. Nevertheless, I would like to express my feelings at this point and something that I had never thought of until now: I had been *robbed.*

Therefore, two very uncanny occurrences took place. With this word, *uncanny*, I am taking the Scottish meaning of the word: First, my cohorts and I were escorted out of Ms. Beauty Pageant's classroom as refuse. Secondly, Ms. Unsightliness had robbed us. In my own evaluation of the situation, most of the third graders would have chosen Ms. Beauty Pageant's classroom to learn. And Ms. Unsightliness probably was not favored with the voting members of the student body of the third grade. Thus, the only method in which to get more students for Ms. Unsightliness was to *rob* them by extraction for any misdemeanor violations. However, on record, this was not a misdemeanor. The crime was recorded as a felony classroom violation needing the utmost punishment on the first day.

Both Ms. Unsightliness and Ms. Beauty Pageant understood *speed*.

As a third grader, I was only being bullied by teachers. The first by her *strictness*. The second by *robbery*.

A third grader by action
Expressing his first amendment rights
Without having learned
Any amendments

A teacher by action
Expressing her willingness to thwart
The first amendment rights
Of a child that knew them not
Two thousand twenty has been a heart-breaking year
Even with the bulldozing of the evidence
Found within its walls
Eastlawn Elementary School
Had been brutally demolished
With the evidence buried

Fourth-Grade-Hood

Upon entrance to fourth grade, my memory started once again. It came alive only, really, at the point of the eye exam that was conducted. The eye exam had been conducted at the first part of the year. It must have been to verify that any and all children in the public school had the proper vision to see the blackboard and any teaching materials. I had been one of those selected in the eye exam.

However, I do question if my eyes could have seen the entire school year for third grade clearly enough. Obviously, as a second or third grader, I would never have realized that my eyesight had been on the decline. I had never felt that at all in any part of my life. Unfortunately, my eyesight had followed the path of my mother's eyes: serious vision deficiencies. Though my parents both wear glasses, my mother's nearsightedness, of which I inherited, without corrective lenses, is like being blind. Thus, though I love swimming, I hate not being able to see until I put corrective spectacles back on out of the water.

Taking the eye exam in the fourth grade, my eyes had failed to pass. Yet, I wonder, did I really have good vision all through third grade? I do not recall one eye exam before that time. I do remember, though, I could read the board when Ms. Unsightliness, the third-grade teacher, had written the word *hate* on the board. I think that word was so clear, it was like seeing it with binocular vision.

Nevertheless, after that other live nightmare—the third one of my life—like a shark pouncing upon its prey, I question my eyesight performance after the trauma experienced due to my sentencing. One thing or another made its impact upon my eyesight. What I experienced in third grade, no child should experience. No child should be left behind in Ms. Unsightliness's classroom! My conclusion is the following: the trauma experienced of being placed in Ms.

Unsightliness's class as punishment, her not adhering to my constitutional rights, and being questioned about my sentencing, affected my vision for schooling.

I failed at keeping a great friend in third grade.

I failed at keeping Ms. Beauty Pageant as my teacher in third grade.

I failed in my explanation of my usage of the word *hate* to Ms. Unsightliness.

My eyes failed during the long enduring process with Ms. Unsightliness in third grade.

I failed the eye exam in fourth grade.

Failures and live nightmares attacked my desire to become highly educated.

I had failed the eye exam. My eyes had suffered. I had gone through a year with an unsightly teacher, receiving as recompense flawed vision.

This is the corrective action I had taken as a primary school student:

1. I became shy.
2. I only looked at the teacher in the classroom and did not turn around.
3. I had made a creative sentence according to my age and according to the unsightly teacher, *I hate my teacher.*
4. I had received spectacles with further punishment in the fourth grade.

I did not realize how serious looking at an ugly teacher all year long could do to one's eyes.

Admission to third grade
Presented renewal for a second dream
A beautiful teacher to inspire education
A newly found friend to affect communication
Reality blackened both eyes
Punishment ensued for communicating with one
Jealousy was the temperament
That destroyed what relationship I could have had
With both the teacher and the friend

Fifth-Grade-Hood:
Lessons for Teachers

My parents had decided for my brother and I to change schools to a Lutheran school for our benefit and our schooling: for me, it was the fifth and sixth grades there. Private Christian schools, as I understand, show students excel more than those at public schools. However, I was not versed in all the reasons why my parents had unanimously selected to decline and yank my membership out of the public school system, but in any case, they had rooted for me to get better and enhanced schooling in a private Christian school.

My memory could grasp a little more by this time: There were certain events that were an obligation from the school to participate in, and there were events decided by the children to participate in. Obviously, every event, in my opinion—that was my own decision—impacted my memory with a more lasting impression in my mind. Could it have been the first time I was given an opportunity to choose events to participate in? I recall not from kindergarten to fourth grade any events within the school term that were voluntary, except those events that were during the summer or during recess.

To this, I would have to sum it up: lasting impressions are those which are voluntary and are from the will of one's own person. The events that were an obligation, the majority of them, obviously, the school work, the tedious assignments, homework, the non-voluntary tasks throughout the school day, were learned, to some extent, but they were pushed out of the memory bank, including, per se, the names of the teachers, the material within the curriculum, any and all daily activities were thus forgotten and dragged into the part of the brain in which these daily activities have been shelved. Albeit, the volunteered activities of the basketball team, the races that I had chosen, the time I had chased the girls, either during recess or at lunch break, are still remembered to this day.

In retrospect, therefore, since I had experiences in third grade, not of my own will, and those that were forced onto me and those that were of punishment were remembered, but the remembrance of these were only negative experiences rather than positive ones. The others, the ones that were voluntary, and of my own will, were positive experiences and those which the mind still has placed in the memory of a positive event.

In addition, to my understanding, the negative experiences had dealt a blow to me not because I had previously been instructed in how to perform; rather, it appears, that as a young lad not wishing in any way, especially at such a young age and very easily molded into a model schoolboy, to extend harm to anyone's person. The only harm I received was, to my own knowledge, because I received no instruction before these occurrences had placed me into a position of receiving punishment. In view of these with a magnifying glass, I was subject to punishment at the very place where I should have been taught! In truth, then, I was punished due to the lack of instruction by the instructress.

That said, this deserves, not litigation, per se, but incorporating what is the Biblical model:

"And these words, which I command thee this day, shall be in thine heart:[7] and thou shalt teach them diligently unto thy children, and shalt talk of them when thou sittest in thine house, and when thou walkest by the way, and when thou liest down, and when thou risest up.[12]"

The biblical model is to teach diligently the commandments or the laws of God. In reference to life, it appears that instruction should be first. If there is no instruction given to someone, how can someone be justly punished?

Does anyone within a city know all the laws that have been written by the legislative body incorporated into law? Do students know all the rules of the school? Some of the rules and a lot of the laws are not known by the public; yet it can be stated with affirmation that all students, per se, and all citizens are mandatorily required to obey the laws of the land.

[12] Deut. 6:6–7.

As a third grader that I was, one could say sentencing for not obeying the rules was given swiftly; yet, in my knowledge, or in my memory recollection, nothing is recalled as regarding when the teachers had provided any instruction regarding the rules. It was also the first day of class for the third grade. No doubt, on the first day of class, rules should be outlined by public school instructors. I assure you, as I know myself, had the instructress pointed out the rules to us before doing anything else, no doubt I would have obliged.

Secondly, for the other instructor, I had been questioned for expressing a feeling. Both were punishments that I had had received, as far as the recollection goes, for not knowing and not being educated beforehand. Yet the teachers were punishing me for their, in my opinion, lack of instilling in me the rules or sense of good behavioral conduct before it took place. Further, would not it be better to give a warning rather than a candid reprimand at that age? Yet the second teacher was, in my opinion, not instilling in me a sense of fulfillment of my own expression but a sense of inhibition towards expressing what I had felt as unjust punishment.

First day of class
Rules unknown
Punished for the teacher's
Lack of instruction
A schoolchild forced to learn
Without a will of one's own
No decisions offered to increase one's learning
Negative experiences are made without choices
Shuffled experiences into oblivion
Positive experiences result from choice
Further building the mind's structure and voice
For the mind and the will together
Build a lasting impression
With memory to recall it all

What comes to mind during these years was the opportunity to play basketball on the school team, even though my stature was short, and the team was the worst in the league. Still, it was an opportunity to get out there and play, have Dad come watch us and take part in community events.

Moreover, more students come to memory in this school than at the other. There was Jeff Lorenz, who happened to have older sisters. There were the twin sisters and Lori Sweebe who loved to have me chase them. And also there was Mr. Kelly's daughter and Jason, the one my brother and I played basketball with. There were a few teachers I vaguely remember. Kelly, Mr. Stern Face and Mrs. Stern Face (These names have been changed so I do not get punished!), who visited our home.

Mr. Stern Face taught a couple of subjects: religion and choir. Somehow he managed to get into teaching religion with a death stare. Just with one look, obedience was the norm for all children.

The elementary teachers should have been excellent instructors. Much was given over to the children, nevertheless, to battle with the science workbook on their own time and in their own homes. In retrospect, the only idea of the curriculum that pops up in my remembrance was that most challenging part of the curriculum: the science workbook had questions that Mom and Dad had no clue for the answers! The only thing my brother and I did to get answers was to bother Mom and Dad with the science workbooks, stating that we could not find the answers. They were, likewise, clueless!

The methodology of the instructors is not recalled. That is, anything at all within all the classrooms from kindergarten through fourth grade, including fifth and sixth grade at a private school in my mind come not with any recollection of any teacher methodology or any instruction at all for that matter, except the classroom work of writing sentences for Ms. Unsightliness and Mr. Stern Face's strict adherence to learning the books of the Bible, reciting them in front of all the students. All the classes that I had to participate in by sitting long hours, listening to lectures about English, science, math, history, even religion have nothing to recall. It's like it has all been wiped clean with a wet tissue! I did recall daydreaming, though, in fifth grade. Even the daydream could be remembered—even to this day (*Jaws*)! However, the content of discussions could not, not even one! It was all erased!

The question comes to mind: Why would all of it just vanish without any recollection of any material at all? Was it the fact that it was forced participation in something I despised and hated deep within? Was it because I had no say in any of the curriculum at all? Was it because I had been mandated not to participate, just listen? Or was it just that my brain was not big enough to put all of it into memory? Participation in assignments was sitting with eyes directly on the material or to the front without any engagement whatsoever with others. Was it that all was such a drab and mandated that nothing could be recollected?

It would seem like there would be some memory recall as to the curriculum or more experiences that would have a lasting impact upon my life or the lives of my other classmates for good. Albeit, the only things remembered were only those most hated experiences, and that is it!

Nothing really outstanding made an impact on my schooling. Only one thing kind of stands out: As I sat in my seat, my mind drifted to the TV programs or movies that I had watched the previous night. In other words, the movies that had consumed my nights had put such an impression on me that during the day in the class, I could not focus on the lesson.

What I dreaded most of all was getting my name called to answer a question from the material in the textbook. If my name was called, what followed was complete silence, insomuch that I felt embarrassed, and the teacher probably did, too.

Moreover, at night, also, trying to read the homework readings, all was so terribly boring and nonsensible that I could not make heads nor tails of it. It was so challenging for me to concentrate on the meaning of the texts. In addition, even reading the Bible during those days was challenging. It was tough to grasp the content with the mind focused on previous movies seen. Nevertheless, that interest in movies, cartoons, and programs on TV was there because it was so easy to just sit in the family room and watch TV. Those images managed to stay on the mind more than anything a textbook could provide, because the difference was, in reading the textbook, I had to literally fight to understand what was written. And I was not shown nor taught how to study: we were just told to read. My guideline for study was to read it once. I was lenient on myself. If I had not grasped the content after one reading, I did not intend nor desire to return to any of the content, but I left it as though it were unimportant!

However, when watching a movie, it was entertaining and easily grasped. Thus, the difference between reading and watching movies was the difference between being fed and having to feed myself by putting in the effort. At that age, since I had had no instruction otherwise, and the content was so much more interesting in the movies or the TV, and I needed not struggle for understanding, that gained not only my time but also my interest while textbooks became the hated forced curriculum. The movies and the TV were selected because they were desired, and it was all voluntary rather than forced onto the will of someone by mandated hourly practice.

Thus, even though the instructress was teaching, the images of movies and TV programs or cartoons raced back into the mind during the instruction from the teacher. I had been looking directly at the teacher, but my mind was elsewhere, in dreamland. The teacher must have assumed I was paying attention, but my mind was so far from the content of the lesson like she was teaching about the Grand Canyon and I was meditating on the movie *Jaws*.

Watching movies for reasons of choice
Was an easy route to information
Though, it made the schoolchild a passive daydreamer
Concentration efforts required double or triple the effort
Robbing the desire for schooling and education
Where the child had no choice or voice
In school, listening to instruction and while reading a textbook
The child really needing a choice and a voice

There were a few things that caused me to be disgruntled about the schooling at the private Lutheran school: First, there was the musician, Mr. Stern Face, who happened to teach music and religion. His face and countenance looked as stern as a bull, and he appeared to take on the aura of an angry villain that his religion was forced upon him. He, therefore, desired to force it upon every student he had. In his quest, he made each student memorize all the books of the Bible and say it in front of the entire class.

Thus, whenever a student failed within his or her memorization, the music/religion teacher must have shaken his head in disgust and thought all the other students made that student embarrassed as quiet chuckles ensued—which actually might have been his goal—to see the students who did not memorize the books squirm before the hearers and onlooker students like, "What is the problem with Linda (or Joe)? Could not they memorize the entire list?"

The torment of those moments was in waiting for one's name to be called. I had the books memorized, so I did not feel a wave of embarrassment overwhelm me. Yet I remember there were a few students who had that embarrassing moment of not being able to recite the entire list or in the heated adrenaline rush forget some. Then the stern eyes of Mr. Stern Face peered back at the student, sending an immediate red blush to the face. I cared not that they did not recite the list, and probably the others cared not either, but they must have felt like being pelted with rocks.

Secondly, there were the science books that Mom and Dad, when asked to assist in explaining the texts with the new scientific terms to our laymen's terms, but they were also stuck in laymen's terms! Their expertise did not qualify them, though the texts were written for primary school children!

Let me digress a bit to include something that I did like though: the basketball team. My dad had encouraged me when I got onto the basketball team to become more aggressive as he saw a winner in me. Of course, at my height, that measured me towards a disadvantage. However, I did take advantage of more usage of the ball and drilling it into the net. It did assist the team, though I knew not how well we fared overall at the end of the season. Usually, our team was one of those that came near the bottom of the list. If we had won a game or two, it may have been out of pure luck.

The third sour point: The Lutheran school had introduced us to soccer playing. That point of soccer playing by force was a distaste in my mouth like having one's mouth washed out with soap. It made not only schooling have an awful distaste to it, but the sport of playing soccer by mandate was like looking over the horizon at a beautiful ocean with crystal clear waters, an extremely beautiful beach and a hot day, but one has to swim in the local swimming pool inside four walls. This was, in fact, introducing a game within America that was not American culture. However, in so doing, it was by mandate by the school—a mandate that made me feel like it was not comfortable. The influence of the international community towards Americans to participate and have a soccer team is the means to give headaches to Americans. To me, Americans, in general, probably 99.9 percent of them do not prefer soccer over football. Well, at least 99.9 percent of boys and dads. However, the international community by sheer force by decree of making America look bad because it does not participate wholeheartedly throughout America in this world-wide approved sport is frowned upon. From Britain to Germany to South America and all of those excellent players and teams of soccer, they wish to make the American team look like shredded beef. In reality, though, the desire of the majority of real Americans are more pro basketball, football, and even baseball more than soccer. Soccer comes in at the bottom of the barrel to normal Americans. Because of the international pressure to participate and be excellent at soccer, the international community has actually influenced the lives of some Americans to participate in a sport that is frowned upon not by the international community but by the real hearts of Americans. If one were to dig deeply into the heart of real genuine Americans, soccer comes in at a very low rate of interest.

The percentage of Americans that watch soccer is at 7 percent[13]. That percentage, no doubt, one could say, is only because of the international people living in America. Therefore, those who like soccer view soccer while true-blooded Americans have their hearts on American football. American football is the number-one sport in America. Statistics, they say, are rising for interest in soccer in America. I think the truth is closer to this reality: As the international community rises, that is, those who come from overseas and bring their soccer interests here, there is a rise in interest only in those expatriates towards soccer. Maybe the international community would like to persuade Americans to participate, but the truth is, their hearts will not and cannot be in it as much as it is in football! Football, to Americans, is the most attractive sport, though; it is also considered the most dangerous.

---

[13] Michael David Smith. "Gallup Poll Shows Football Overwhelmingly Americans' Favorite Sport." NBCSports. January 10, 2018. Retrieved June 21st from https://profootballtalk.nbcsports.com/2018/01/10/gallup-poll-shows-football-overwhelmingly-americans-favorite-sport/.

Therefore, when the Lutheran school during PE had us children play a game of soccer, all the children became involved by force. I was distraught. My heart flipped. I grew to hate soccer. I am not sure how the other children felt, but my feelings were in disgust. Thus, I am putting the blame on the Lutheran school for having tried to instill a liking towards soccer which was never and would never be in the heart. Soccer is not culturally American. It has never been, and it should never become culturally American. Though soccer has possibly four billion fans around the world, that and that alone is the reason why the pressure is on for America to step up to the bat and become part of the international soccer community. The reality is, though, Americans, if one digs deep enough, do not have the same ideal for soccer. Further, as true Americans as we are, keenly interested in football, basketball, or baseball, being influenced by the international community, to have soccer become an American sport should be halted. The only reason is the pressure from the international community to push Americans into their soccer uniforms. The international community is like the referee saying to the American players: "Go get your uniform on and play! "However, when parents realize that their children are being persuaded by the PE teacher to play more and more soccer, American parents need to write their congressmen and protest against the school system's manipulation! Soccer needs to be moved overseas; the American flag should only have our sports on it! All soccer fields should be required to be changed to football fields only!

It is outrageous to think that the Americans who participate in the soccer sport are only heeding to international demands for competition of the sport that the international community view is their top interest. Since most Americans do not like soccer, why force the issue? Why try to make soccer culturally American when the sport is only played at the behest of the international community? The heart of Americans still strives for football, not soccer. Football is the sport that is loved the most by Americans!

Therefore, in that one game of soccer on the Lutheran school field, though playing, even with girls included, I grew to hate it because it was by force of the school staff to succumb to the pressures of the international community to make America change its sports culture to include soccer. It just does not fit, so why make it fit? Why was I playing soccer? Was it to heed to the pressure cooker of the international community? Was it commanded by the UN?

My mom and dad, being Americans and Lutherans did not instill, in any way, a love for soccer. That never crossed our minds to even discuss it!

International community desires
To push soccer in American schools
By mandate without a choice
To make America change sports culture
To a sport all other countries understand
And not come without that desire
To have soccer be the first of the land
But Americans we will be
Our sports culture will remain
Uniquely American
To the stadium with cheering fans

One day, the Lutheran school fifth grade teacher came to visit our home. I remember that day so clearly. I remember exactly what her face looked like. She was not old, probably in her thirties, also thin, and acted like a strict teacher, a really strict one. I was hesitant. Teachers can be mean.

And, so it was. When she had become my teacher at the Lutheran school and class had ended for the day, and so my studies did, too, I thought we had all gotten into a line just outside the classroom for inspection to return home. She had seen me without any books in my hand. I was caught. I was told to return into the classroom to retrieve my spelling book. I needed to learn spelling at home. She pushed the teaching off onto me to learn by myself. I thought she had explained to my parents that she was a great teacher and willing to teach. Why, then, was she pushing her duties of teaching onto me by giving me a lot of homework and making me stuff my spelling book into my bag? It was not the question of my will but a question of obedience to the teacher who was pushing her duty onto me. From that moment on, I had lost confidence in her as a great teacher.

"Obey them that have the rule over you, and submit yourselves: for they watch for your souls, as they that must give account, that

they may do it with joy, and not with grief: for that is unprofitable for you."[14]

For schoolchildren, it is profitable to study and to obey the teacher, though I really did not want to carry my book all the way home. It was about a thirty-minute walk home, and I was not thinking about spelling. In fact, the spelling book just had a different resting place for the night. It still ended up not being opened until the next class we had spelling.

There were two people from the Lutheran school that I will comment on: One, the son of Mr. Stern Face, the music teacher, and the other, I will disguise his name, I shall call him Alex. Alex was a friend of mine. He and I would walk home from school together. His home was closer than mine, so I had to walk a substantial way home even after saying goodbye to him. One of the things that he had, though, was a tongue that was like a serpent's tongue. That is, in the class, there would come out of his tongue, obviously, because of the influence of the teachers, nothing derogatory. Albeit, outside of the school and on the way home, he introduced swearing to me: it was like he used the vocabulary from the mud. He wiped it on his tongue when he got out of school and started blurting it out like spit, and it got all over everywhere he talked, on the sidewalk, the trees, the plants and the grass. Pretty soon, the plants were dying, the sidewalk was cracked, and the trees were losing their leaves.

It was as though he had he wanted to share the serpent's tongue with me. Thus, he reached down into his mouth, pulled out his tongue, and shoved it into my mouth without my permission or my request. And that is why he had a forked tongue. One of the sides of his tongue, he gave to me and the other he kept. Thus, I began the same type of rant. After school I learned more from spitting mud than in the school getting bored with textbooks I hardly looked at.

However, one day, there was a brief price tag that I had to pay. Mr. Stern Face's son was outside of the school, too, and for some odd reason, memory fails to recall, I began a rant of using my tongue with mud on it to spit some out at Mr. Stern Face's son. That is, I started cussing at him. He was not too pleased with my tongue usage, so he came over by me and used his fist to implant it into my glasses. My glasses were knocked off my face, and one lens, at least, was broken. Because of this occurrence, and my parents having to foot

---

[14] Heb. 13:17

the bill, I had to explain to them what had happened. Thus, we were visited by Mr. Stern Face and his son. The discussion of the two parties were looking for apologies, probably both from Mr. Stern Face's son and me, too.

Lunchhood

During the summer, my dad had expressed to us boys, my older brother and I, that God had told him to change churches. That news did not bother me. For a young lad, curiosity gets the best of them. I wondered about the other church and how it would be. The two younger siblings, the two girls who had come into our home later in our lives, had not been born yet. God had given us grace for a while. This is why God spoke to Dad more often during those days, too.

I remember the meeting place: It was our breezeway. We were having lunch during our summer break when Dad began a meeting during our lunch. The lunch must not have been that important, because I do not remember what we had been eating, but I do remember the concept of the thoughts that he had provided, which he stated had come from God. Thus, upon hearing that, I knew I had to listen intently. Funny how that one remembers the conversation, at least bits and pieces, but one does not have any clue as to what the menu entailed that day. This must be the reason why Jesus had stated not to worry for the morrow of the things one might eat or drink, but one should put the kingdom of God first.[15] I'm not sure, though, why we had started eating first before Dad talked to us about changing churches. In any case, I did not have any say in the matter whether I wanted to change churches. In retrospect, though, I think it was important to do so to boycott soccer playing at the Lutheran school.

He said that he had to take us to a different church. He did not ask for us to vote. He had explained it in a way that he felt it was the will of God. Thus, for school, I still attended the sixth grade at St. John's Lutheran, but our family began attending the Assembly of God congregation in Midland, Michigan. I felt, then,

---

[15] Matt. 6:33

like I was attending two churches, one during the week and one on the weekend. One was Pentecostal and the other Lutheran, so I had become *Penteran*.

Thus, my early teenage years had Pentecostal preaching involved in it. I had remembered some preaching about the gifts of the Spirit, and there were those who had invited us to pray at the altar. That was something new, praying at the altar. I did not go to the altar at that age, though. I turned around in my pew and prayed with my head to the pew. I am glad nobody, as far as I can remember, had diarrhea.

"Then will I go unto the altar of God, unto God my exceeding joy: yea, upon the harp will I praise thee, O God my God."[16]

---

[16] Ps. 43:4

Churchhood

One Pentecostal preacher, after his sermon was over, it was said, became drunk in the spirit. That is, he was acting as though he were drunk, though he had drunk no alcohol. **"And be not drunk with wine, wherein is excess; but be filled with the Spirit."**[17]

Those days with some Pentecostal preaching about the Holy Spirit had instructed me much. They were more exciting than the teachers at school. The teachers at school were boring, but the Pentecostal preachers had perked up my spirit.

By that time, I had become a teenager. Even Pentecostal preachers had to get closer to God to convince teenagers to repent and change their rebellious ways. It was harder for preachers and parents than for teenagers. Teenagers grow a bit cold, listening to rock music, drinking on the weekends, going out to parties and such, then coming to church on the weekend too. It is their long hair that gives them away. Pentecostal preachers, then, because of the coldness that teenagers feel as the result of their lifestyle, either in parties, drinking, or even drugs, must seek God wholeheartedly, coming up with a distinct message from God for teenagers to feel the conviction upon their hearts and the wind of the Holy Spirit leading them to repentance. If the preacher does not get closer to God and the power of the Holy Spirit, the teenager may just brush it all off and become an atheist by the time he is a university student.

---

[17] Eph. 5:18

Little Leaguehood

One thought I had in mind was this: One day I want to be a baseball player. That was my occupational goal as a young lad. To realize this, I needed to practice and get involved in the little leagues. Instead of getting on a football team, baseball team, basketball team, or getting involved in wrestling at school, I set my sights on little league baseball. It did not involve getting coached by the same coaches at school, and it did not involve the same young lads at school, either. Thus, it gave me a sense of freedom from seeing the same people in school and outside of school, and a sense of freedom from the same teachers, also.

Tryouts were hardly remembered. Somehow I had managed to get on the team and tried out for a particular position, and somehow, without any memory of trying out for any other positions besides possibly short stop, I had become the catcher. I probably would have preferred short stop, but for some reason, I got what I thought was the worst position, sitting behind the plate, having to sit awkwardly, watching the ball being thrown at full speed towards my mitt. I rarely missed the ball unless it was an extremely wild pitch. Jim Baker, who was on our team and the best pitcher we had, was not wild. Sometimes, the other pitchers were a tad wild now and then. Jim Baker, however, kept it steady.

It just seemed that the players had chosen what they wanted to do, and I got stuck with what no one else wanted to do. That seemed to be the things I got in life: everything that nobody else wanted to do was what I had to do. Catching was just a little inconvenient. As a catcher, one has the most equipment one must put on his body, and the mask makes it troublesome to see everything going around. One must always pay attention to the baseball, and especially the runner on first base if there is one. That is what I dreaded the most. If the player on first base steals second base, the catcher feels a bit of embarrassment, because the throw to second base makes the catcher look great or embarrassed. If it was off or wild or the player ran faster than my throw, though I was not a pitcher, my emotions would take a beating and the parents of the other players would frown upon my bad team playing.

Thus, I dreaded it, but I never mentioned it. I just acted as though I was a great thrower of the ball to second base and that I could handle it. However, I do not remember me getting the players out when they stole second base. Had I remembered, I probably would have thought of myself as a better catcher, but the only reason why I was a good catcher was due to the baseballs ending up in my mitt instead of on the grass behind home plate.

That task of throwing to second base to stop a player stealing a base was the most hated memory of that position. I hated throwing the ball to second base because of a thief trying to steal a base. That act in my life was the closest that I got to acting like a policeman! I was enforcing the law by throwing the ball to the second base to stop the player stealing a base. I dreaded it deep inside of my being! I just do not like stealing. In fact, stealing is against the law! Though, I chose not to become a policeman, I feel stealing is taking what is rightfully someone else's! Second base does not belong to stealers of bases! Thus, as the catcher, I was trying to enforce the law to keep that player off second base, which was not his!

One dreaded task of a catcher
To throw the ball to second base
All because of a thief
Who wishes to steal a base
Once I threw the ball to second base
The parents began to realize
Why I was not a pitcher
For my throw was not precise

During little league, on the team called Dick Blasy Sport and Bike, because of the players that were on that team, that team had become awesome! We had such pitchers as Jim Baker, Matt Rapanos, Matt McPhillips, and others. The best, obviously, was Jim Baker. He always struck out players and kept the game mostly in our favor. The others were average pitchers, but I was always happy to see Jim on the plate pitching. When the other pitchers were on the mound, sometimes they made it, and other times, the other team gained runs. For me, that might have been the second most thing I disliked about being a catcher: having to stay longer behind the plate because the pitcher was mediocre. From the mediocre pitchers came some wild pitches. Secondly, the ball may not have passed into my glove; instead, it sailed to the outfield, sometimes bringing in runners to home plate. And I was supposed to tag them, but the ball was not on its way. That put more pressure upon me as a catcher, too, because the pitchers that were not the best always had players on base. The inning lasted longer; the players in the outfield worked harder, because the pitcher was run of the mill. Our parents were not happy; everyone on our team felt more tension and ill at ease. That made me work harder by throwing the ball to second base more often, too. Thus, the best thing to do is always do one's best to help the entire team. If one slouches as a pitcher, it makes the entire team suffer!

Thus, my mind always wished for Jim Baker to be on the mound! Sometimes I wished I could be the coach and make that decision myself, but the coaches sometimes made bad decisions for the entire team! There was something about the way Jim Baker threw the ball that made it harder for the hitter to hit. He struck out more players while the other pitchers allowed more hit balls. Therefore, the other team was always waiting and wishing for our coaches to make bad decisions, and having the mediocre pitcher get up there to pitch and make life easier for them. I got embarrassed about two things: runs came in and players advanced to second base due to runners stealing bases. Thus, my inside prayer was for the coach to make a change to Jim Baker, but he was the starting pitcher and would not replace the other ones. So, I had to deal with more pitched balls, a longer inning, and a longer embarrassing game.

Thus, Jim Baker and I were good friends, not only because he lived right next door to us, but also because he made catching much easier and less of an embarrassment for the team and for me. If Jim Baker is out there somewhere reading this, I would like to thank him for making our team the best team! He saved us embarrassment, and he pitched well to annoy and mortify the other team! Thank you, Jim Baker, for making our lives better by pitching well to win games and not getting us angry and feeling ill on the way home! Hence, Jim Baker helped make our team one of the best in the leagues!

A pitcher makes a big difference
For the entire team
From the catcher to the left fielder
If the pitcher does a great job
It signals a better team
And maybe games that can be won

A mediocre pitcher
Throwing wild and crazy
Signals bad luck for the team
Hit balls, home runs and runs
Make for a loss of a game
And a loss of motivation

My batting average was stupendous also on this team. In fact, I would say that I was a part of the untouchables of the team, which meant I had prestige. One could say I was among the top four, at least. Jim did an awesome job at pitching, but he was just all right at batting. He was probably the first one at bat. I came in at third or fourth, though I rarely hit a home run. I did hit often and moved players from one base to the next.

My mind returns to an event that had occurred during the baseball season and during practice. We had practice now and then, not too often and not rarely. The assistant coach, a man with a beard, always wearing a hat, was nice, not grumpy, not overzealous, just a plain coach who liked the team and the players. However, my life as a young man was a bit mischievous. At times, I got a little beyond the borders of playfulness. There was, on the team, an African American. In Midland, especially during those days, Black children in school or even on our team were so rare. He was the only one. He was very tall, and his demeanor was pleasant. There was nothing outstanding about his character, his mannerisms, or anything out of the ordinary. He seemed to want to fit in with the rest, and he did. No one treated him any different. It just so happened, though, one day, I made myself a nitwit. I mistreated this Black boy with words that, to an African American, were like cuss words.

Inwardly, I felt no hate, no dislike at all towards Black people. Even at that age, everything was a blank page. I was probably thirteen to fourteen years of age at that time, looking for fun. Then, it came out. "Nigger!" I began calling him that bad cuss word type of a name, but I did not do it because I felt any ill feelings towards him, or towards any Black person at all for that matter. The only reason I said it was to have fun, even though I know not the name of the African American boy who played with us during those days. I knew not much about him, then, nor do I to this day. I did not know where he lived, and nothing about his family or his private life. I did not even know how he felt about it. I just thought I would have some fun, so I called him a nigger. Everything was fine until the coach heard what I had said.

As previously mentioned, I thought I was in the untouchable league, that is, part of the group of that team that was so necessary, so needful by the coach and by the team that any kind of behavior like that would never disqualify me from playing at all. The truth is, I must have been a little narrowminded at the time. I'm not sure the boys were laughing. I did not even feel that that Black boy felt any ill will towards me for it, either. When I said it, nothing in my conscience flared stating that I should never have said it. However, the coach's conscience must have riled him up.

It was not the bearded assistant coach that said anything. It was the main coach, the man who did not wear a beard. Did I get along with any of the coaches? I thought the bearded coach was more personable, but the other coach was just another coach, and a tad sterner, by the way. Anyway, the un-expected words of shock I heard were, "You are off the team!"

Those were cuss words to me! Those were words I did not want to hear, nor did I expect to hear. It probably even jolted the entire team when the coach said that to me. In any case, it was justice being done to me for my bad mouthing!

To hear that, I became a little daunted in my outlook on life. Why would he kick me off the team? Was what I said so detrimental to the boy and to everyone else that it made that much of a negative impression? I thought I was part of the team that was untouchable, but I was sadly mistaken. Of course, I had no ill feelings towards the Black boy and only said it out of having a good time, but the coach must have been thinking about his family, the Black boy's feelings, and the overall perspective if that had become news to the society at large that a Black boy had been called that cuss word at practice.

The team was going to play some difficult teams in the near future, and we all felt bad concerning what had happened. I do believe that the coach had asked me to apologize to the Black boy. I believe I did without any misgivings. Certainly, I meant no harm, just a way to make practice a little more exciting for us, but my idea was not looked upon as being enlightening for a practice. The coach hammered down on me.

I was suspended for a period of probably three games. After that, everything was back to normal. The head coach felt I had been punished enough. After that incident, I have never called any Black person that cuss word. It has never crossed my lips, not even once since. Since I believed I apologized and got punished from that event, to this day I have never called anyone else that cuss word. In fact, if I ever hear that word being said about a Black man, I do not condone its practice. To the contrary, I think it reprehensible for anyone to say it.

In little league practice
Wanting to have some fun
Out came a word that is not condoned
I quickly learned

Punished again without any prior instruction
As to what harm it may have caused
Not knowing the boy, his family, nor anything about him
Just trying to have some fun
Which was not condoned

Flaghood

However, let me expound some of my outrage, though. Since I was disciplined by the coach who had suspended me for three games, I had learned a lot through that experience that abruptly changed my outlook on saying such a word. I was a young schoolboy needing education and instruction in the ethics of life.

However, let me turn to something I think is required to look much further and deeper into what I call real outrage. I was just a plain schoolboy, needing a lesson or instruction before it happened, really. My outrage views something that is portrayed in a state south of us by those who have political pull, but it just does not seem comprehensible in any way that part of the flag of a state is that of the Confederate flag (I had written this prior to June 30, 2020, when the flag was pulled)!

To me, displaying any part of the Confederate flag is a push towards more animosity, more hatred, and more thoughts of what it represents and what it represented during the Civil War. The whole push of the Civil War for the south was to keep Blacks in slavery. Thus, it represents a symbol of slavery; yet to my astonishment, it still flies in Mississippi! To my surprise—this is the year 2020—165 years *after* the Civil War had ended! There is still a part of a flag of a state, the Mississippi flag, that contains part of the Confederate flag!

Any display, in my opinion, of the Confederate flag presents a serious infraction of civility and ethics. To some, they might think it looks cool, but to display something that engenders racism in a symbol, that is not cool! During the Civil War, the Confederate flag flew for the purpose of slavery, keeping Blacks as slaves. To fly the Confederate flag today in the South just does not symbolize harmony and encouragement towards African Americans. Instead, it feeds the minds of the African Americans and Whites that there is no sense of justice, peace, and respect from the Confederate flag. How can that flag even be flown? Some say it is their voice or the right to free speech. Is it not hate speech? Is it not racism? The reason for free speech is to voice complaints against some group of people that are not getting their rights heard by the majority of people; yet this is seemingly a voice to speak their minds against having freedom for all. Is it not a voice that clamors for slavery? Is it a voice that gives justice to all? Is not it a voice or a symbol towards disrespect of a race in America? Is it not a voice that says we wish the silence and the animosity towards the African American community?

The Confederate flag represents to the society the mindset of the South in the time right before the Civil War. Ultimately, the Confederate flag has a symbol of this idea: Blacks need to return to slavery; therefore, it is worse than that cuss word I said that day! Furthermore, during that time of the Blacks being in slavery, that derogatory cuss word must have been utilized more than at any other time. Thus, words belittled them and the action of holding them as non-citizens, working as slaves belittled them much further! As time progressed, that term was erased from the tongue of the learned or civilized society and then slowly, from others too as the Blacks became African Americans, citizens with rights!

However, I am irate, not because I learned such a valuable lesson as a young lad, but in realizing that in America, there is still a symbol of slavery being flown as the state flag of Mississippi! Yet I had no idea of that flag flying in Mississippi for numerous years of my life, possibly also many, many others who knew nothing of that previous state flag! How callous can this be towards those we should give the same respect to today? Portraying the Confederate flag in part of the flag of Mississippi is likened to keeping slavery and the derogatory terms for African Americans intact. Worse than the cold cuss word being thrown at them, the symbol of the Confederate flag is like advertising for African Americans to return to the bondage of slavery! Those who feel the need to display such a flag are exhibiting animosity, incivility, and cold heartedness towards the African American community. Truly, it is a sad state of affairs when Confederate flags are flown by the voluntary will of any true-blooded American. It is like saying slavery needs to return.

Mississippi needs a flag change
To lead America in the right direction
Forgetting those symbols of racism and hate
Stirring up a better model for the mindset
Of inclusion and not offense
To citizenship and not the sense
Of an enslaved past
(Flag had descended, June 20, 2020!)

That event, of calling the Black boy that infamous cuss word, taught me to watch my tongue, especially for racist remarks in the future. I did not know that such a vocabulary word was prohibited. It was a learning experience by having to face the consequences of that which I did not know was wrong. Soon, though, I had felt the weight of the coach's conscience nail me like a hammer! Though it was tough not going to the three games I missed and playing with, what I believed, the best team, that event instructed me more about what real bad behavior or a bad mouth could do to have others react against offenses caused. For me, my bad mouth caused me to miss out on what I really wanted to experience, being with a great team and having the opportunity to play baseball with them, even the African American boy. Nevertheless, truly, I had learned my lesson: never again would I allow anything like that to come out of my mouth, realizing the hurt I had caused the African American boy, the sense of not leading others to say the same cuss words, and the way not to receive punishment for my mouth's ill behavior.

Thus, in retrospect, not once has that cuss word crossed my lips again.

Sorryhood

And I want to write to the African American boy that was on our team: If I did not apologize to you on that day, I want to apologize today. I am terribly sorry for having said that. It must have been embarrassing for you! Now that I am older, I can understand a little how it must have felt that you, as the only African American person on the team, were sidelined and mocked as if I had put a knife in your back. That word must have been a killer against your inner motivation and the learning of civics, ethics, and friendship in America. Thus, I apologize to you for it, here and now. Secondly, I apologize to all African Americans for having had to go through some of that same experience from others that may not have understood how you felt being called that dirty, racist word.

Pure Midlandhood

Essentially, that is what it is. Today, African Americans have experienced a better citizenship because slavery has been abolished, equal rights have been pursued, and that word that drives a knife in their back has been dealt with. For some, they may use it in jokes, not realizing that in doing so, it may engender racism, but I have not heard this type of joke for so many, many years, making me prouder of being an American! To me, that type of joke is demeaning, belittling, indignant, and debasing, not offering the sense of dignity that all African Americans deserve. Further, all jokes should never belittle any race, for it leads to a seed of racism.

"*Let* nothing *be* done through strife or vainglory; but in lowliness of mind let each esteem other better than themselves.⁴ Look not every man on his own things, but every man also on the things of others.⁵ Let this mind be in you, which was also in Christ Jesus.¹⁸"

Racist words
That cut at the heart
Should be forsaken and not used
For the building of a better society
Of love, kindness, and ethics

That experience was shocking to me. Thinking that I was doing nothing wrong at the time, I found myself severely scolded. Nevertheless, truly, I agree that it was wrong, obviously. Now older, I could never imagine such a word

---

¹⁸ Phil. 2:3–5

coming out of my mouth. Nevertheless, being so young and not knowing the ramifications and the whole perspective of thoughts surrounding that word towards African Americans, it had been quite an eye-opening, learning experience.

In retrospect, the reason why I had not known that it would cause trouble is because we lived in Midland, Michigan. In Midland, there might have been one or two Black children I had seen in school. I had never heard of any cases where the Black children were called any names or given any trouble at all due to their race. In fact, it was purely clean, I shall say. To me, not one Asian, African American, or even a Hispanic that might have graced our school system, to my knowledge, had ever faced any kind of racism or bullying, and that was in the public school.

That said, I was the only one during my entire childhood that said something ill towards a person of a different skin color. That is it! Just me! I was the bad guy! I was the bully! However, the African American that I had said that word to was really a lot taller than I! In retrospect, my intentions were not at all to induce any harm, neither was it to make a bad impression nor cause the team harm. It was done in a mischievous manner, but my intentions were not to provoke anyone to anger or harm anyone's feelings. Nevertheless, I was the only one to *blame* for having said something to an African American in that way. I sincerely do apologize, and I did apologize to him (I believe). I think I was made to apologize by the coach.

That event and pondering about it brings me to this idea: In Midland, though few people were of other races, and having grown up in Midland, in the public school system for the most part, I had never heard of any ill feelings towards any of any other race nor heard of any problems regarding it. It was unheard of. Thus, the coach must have been shocked that it came out of the mouth of one of his team members! He also may have never heard it from any team members at all before! The only one, possibly, in his entire career in Midland that said anything like it was me! Therefore, he had to react and act quickly. The hammer had to come down quickly and sharply!

Like a jolt of electricity
It came from my mouth
Thinking to incite a fun time
Instead, the result from the coach
Was like a cannon bolt
To silence my mouth
Who dared bring
Such a revolting word to a beautiful town
Such as this

Northeast Intermediatehood

My memory at Northeast Intermediate School (grades seven to nine during those days) in Midland, Michigan, had placed more into it than the grade school, per se, but the experiences, really, at the grade school, the private Lutheran school I should emphasize, were better, except for playing soccer.

I was clean then. I did not smoke, drink, party, or do drugs. Those experiences were reserved only for high school and at the ages of sixteen to seventeen.

During this period of public schooling, there were scheduled dances, though, that inwardly, I felt they might have been stretching it concerning what God would want me to do. Rock music was the biggest battle for the mind at that time, along with TV and the movies. It was during those early youth days, the churches I had attended and my parents with one voice had clamored that rock music was not beneficial to listen to; however, they clamored little about the movies—except those that had an excess of violence—because they themselves were participants in the watching of movies. However, they were not participants in listening to rock music, not in the slightest. Yet it was not just this fact that they had stated that rock music was a poor source of music to listen to; it had lyrics that were degrading, and images were placed in the mind that were leading the youth down a path towards evil action.

It was not until I was past the age of fifteen that my girlfriend at the time and I visited a rock concert. It was my first and last rock concert that I had attended. As I recall, neither my girlfriend nor I consumed any alcoholic beverages, did drugs nor had we even smoked cigarettes there, either. It was just the music alone and the fascination of seeing these extraordinary singers on stage. Amongst the crowd, though, one notes that there was the aroma of cigarette smoke and possibly even marijuana that the youth had consumed, besides being a bit tipsy from drinking, some of them. And the music was so extremely loud coming from their speakers that it made sense to back away for the health of one's eardrums.

Was it that the music was introducing vanity into a youth's life? Was it portraying some sounds that were conducive to encouraging actions of the base nature? Most of the discussion from parents were negative towards the listening of rock music. Sometimes, even, parents had to deal with the loudness of the music coming within their teenagers' bedrooms.

One day at Northeast Intermediate School on a Friday night, they had a dance. I went in as shy a boy as I was and stood next to my friend, Tim Warmbier. We were afraid to ask any of the girls for a dance. However, I did finally get my boldness up. It was not the prom but a more informal dance with some '70s rock 'n' roll. The faster songs made the girls dance bumping their hips together. At least, that is how Debbie Ruffing was dancing with a friend of hers. I planned to ask Debbie for a dance. I thought I could show Tim how asking a girl for a dance was done, making a question that would influence her to positively accept by a gentleman like me. I walked over to her since I liked her appearance and popped the question.

"Excuse me. Will you dance with me?" I made my move.

With what appeared to be a snarl on her face, the reaction of which I felt like a ton of cold ice hitting my chest, "No," said Debbie.

And that was it. I was done for the night. With a red face, though it was dark enough not to see the appearance of red in the gym, I walked back over to a smiling Warmbier, who seemed to be saying, "You should not have even asked." And, "I'm glad I didn't ask anyone!"

I intended not to ask anyone else nor return to any more dances at Northeast. That rejection was my formal rejection for returning to any more dances.

Mischievous Iceballhood

As I got older, I began getting deeper into more mischievous teenage events. For example, the thrill of throwing snowballs at cars made us doubly excited when it was possible to pack the snow and observe the reaction of drivers. At least, for me it did. Surely, the drivers of the cars may not have desired snowballs pouncing on their cars; however, when it was an impact with ice, that brought irritation to another level! Most drivers do not stop; others stop, and when they do, the adrenaline rush comes into the legs of the teenagers to get out of dodge!

At the ages of fifteen to sixteen, hanging out a bit with my brother and a neighborhood friend by the last name of Postma, we decided to throw snowballs at cars one night across the park from our home. The meeting place for snowballing was at a house that nobody lived in and was up for sale. Because the house was open to the public for view, we did enter to look around. Then near the street, we picked up snow to peg cars off. The excitement was aroused even further at my curiosity of clobbering a car with an ice ball instead of a snowball. This time, I would clobber the car, but all present in the actions of throwing snowballs, or intending to do so, would be charged collectively for community irritation.

That was my idea, and I thought it an awesome one! Why not walk alongside the sidewalk, wait for a car, and heave it only about a six feet distance away from the car, making it an even greater impact at close range? My mind took affirmative action and decided in favor of it. I consulted not with my brother and Reese. Instead, I just went ahead on my own determination to find a nice big ice ball and made the decision to heave it at close range, getting a reaction from the car owner and my brother and Reese. There was no discussion about it nor was there any argument. They did not know anything about the ice ball

I picked up. However, it was, in my mind, one of the beauties of youthhood, to enjoy some unilateral decisions.

I was walking along the sidewalk very slowly to get a feel of the size of the ice ball and its dimensions, how the ice ball might implant its mark on the side of the car with a sound that not the snowball throwers nor the driver nor any occupants of the vehicle could misinterpret. I patently waited while walking for a car-sized victim to pass in the lane nearest me. My conclusion was, as it was a first for me of this kind, to manhandle the ice ball perfectly as the sunshine for a sunny day, ripe for the occasion.

As I recall, I had only done this once, and the reaction from the driver made the experience a lasting impression upon all of us! This would not be unintelligible handling, but it would be understood from the moment the snowball landed precise on impact, enhancing the thrill of a more distraught driver and the intensity for the others at that explosion of a sound to wring their ears and shock them into awe at my dauntlessness.

There are a few things I had not thought about the snowballing practice as a teenager, though. It is a grand and fun experience, but one must aim only for the body and not for the windows. Secondly, today, there are people who carry guns in their cars and kids have been shot at for snowballing cars.[19] However, back in the day, when I was a teenager, that practice, obviously, was unheard of; hence, it was my lucky break.

Unbeknownst to me, the next car that passed by would be a perfect victim target, not for practice but for real! I was walking along the sidewalk with the snowball conveniently tucked out of sight from the driver and the other collaborators in youth *crime*. We assumed that throwing snowballs at cars was not a crime and were not intending to damage any car. Snow was not about to land me in a youth detention center. I was facing the same direction as the car, waiting for it to come up to parallel position to me. Once it was there, I turned towards the car, manhandled the ice ball by lifting my arm for pitcher practice, and heaved it with my entire muscle like it was dynamite into the side of the car! A loud cracking bang was the next sound

---

[19] Derrick Bryson Taylor. "Two Milwaukee Children Shot After Throwing Snowballs at Cars, Police Say." *The New York Times*. January 7, 2020.
http://www.nytimes.com/2020/01/07/us/milwaukee-snowball-shooting.html.

coming from the car, like a rock exploding on impact! Startled, upset a bit, agitated, nervous, and adrenalized, our boots dug into the snow and started running as fast as our legs could take us.

That tremendous KABOOM was horrendously loud upon impact! It was so loud that it must have startled the driver as well as my companions and me! I not only pegged the car with a monstrous ice ball, but the car, shockingly, also came to a sudden sliding halt! The absolute excitement of hearing the massive impact was immediate glee on our part! Yet the glee was mixed with fear as the car skid to a halt in the middle of the street. The driver opened the door like he was also in the race, got out of the car, and hightailed it directly towards ALL OF US!

Since it had already gotten dark by that time, that was to our youth advantage. No attention was paid by us to the brand name of the car, whether the car was expensive or cheap, whether the car had full occupancy or just one lone driver. I had just seen the lights coming toward us, and one does not judge pitching the ice ball at a car by how many occupants are in the car or if the car is expensive. One only sees the lights, and the car is hardly noticed. From the time the arm is in a cocked position ready to send the ice ball, there is no thought, especially as a youth, whether the car should not receive some loud bang on its door! The jitters were there as a result from the nervousness I had felt. Yet it was not that intense.

In retrospect, walking in the same direction as the car, and turning to heave the ice ball with all my momentum and power, was the easiest way to blast a car at close range. The driver of the vehicle also would not have expected it at all since I did not look as though I was throwing snowballs at cars. The immediate halt of the car was just that: The decision had to be made by the driver in a split second. For the driver to halt the vehicle as fast as possible and hightail it towards us in hot pursuit was bravo of the man. It was three youths against one, but knowing my brother, myself, and Reese, we would never think of threatening him or challenging the man to a duo at all. Instead, he threatened us just by the fact that he stopped and got out of the vehicle, running towards us with all his momentum! The jitters we had felt got worse knowing that the man was after us and only probably five feet from Reese, the third in line in the race!

I have no idea, as to this day, where that ice ball is. My heart goes out to it as it helped me become brave in front of my peers. The others had not even yet tossed one snowball at a car before my plan was thought up and realized! I was the first to heave one, and at such a close range, including using packed ice for sound effects! If I could write a letter to the ice ball, or even thank the ice ball for making my youth have vitality with it in my life, I would do so. However, the ice or water that it is now, one of the witnesses of my courage, has drifted away, maybe down the street, into the sewage and on into a river. The ice ball itself probably had the best time too, being used by me to give it some excitement as well, for sitting on the side of the road being spattered on by slosh or stepped on by feet would have made the ice ball feel useless. However, that day, it must have thought itself privileged, higher than the other ice and snow around it!

My thanks to the ice ball would in no way please the driver. Only revenge dangled into his eyes as he moved his legs as fast as they could go towards us. The driver had probably never thought of outlawing ice balls. Maybe it would be a great idea, though, for him to contact his local congressman and plead to get rid of ice during the winter to save cars from being impacted. It was Reese, though, and not the ice ball that he was after, since he was the slow runner and the one that the driver could pounce on like a lion after its prey! The driver did not even grab the one who had thrown the ice ball, though. Why would Reese be the one that the driver chased if he were not the guilty one? The driver had not gotten me, so I do not know why he was trying to take out revenge upon an innocent boy. Secondly, he did not pick up the evidence of the ice ball, so it would not even stand up in court! Besides that, the ice ball was on my side! And there were three boys' testimony against one driver's testimony. How could we get prosecuted? Third, he could not grab all three of us, but only Reese, an innocent boy, who fell prey to his deadly grip! That was his injustice against Reese! The driver should have been after the ice ball! And he should have been after me, I suppose, but he could not run fast enough, so he had no court case. The only thing that he could do is rat on us to our parents! That was the end of having a private night!

The slow runner, Reese, was interrogated mercilessly. Who was he? Where was his home and his family? Who were his parents and who were the partners-in-crime? Where did the partners-in-crime live?

My brother was as swift as an eagle. He made the longest strides, like a cheetah running from a lion, and he got off to the best start. I managed to be in front of Reese, just behind my brother. My brother was not looking back for the life of him! I only heard and later firsthand saw that Reese had gotten caught.

How the driver caught Reese, I do not know. Whether he commanded the teenager to stop and he stopped or whether he knocked him down or grabbed his arm is a mystery yet to me. All I know is that because he was not like a rabbit getting away from the driver, all our parents were to hear the trouble we got into. The first thing he probably did was rat on us, told the driver exactly where we lived and visited them as soon as he could. The thing that we would hear from our parents was that we were grounded for a very long time!

My brother, out in front, had crossed the entire park and crossed the street on the other side like a jackrabbit, totally free after passing that street beyond the park. I was right behind him and had crossed the park, too, but thought I would not cross the street onto the other side. I assumed I was free being on the park's side of the street. Postma, the caught distraught youth, had to walk with the driver searching for a short while for us around the houses on the other side of the park.

I assumed I was safe not crossing the street but stayed by the houses that were on the park's side. At a particular house I got to, I went just behind a bush and sat down waiting, listening, getting back my breath and passing the time.

Pretty soon, I was hearing a conversation between two people. One sounded like Postma and the other was, shockingly, an undercover cop! The driver of the vehicle was an undercover cop that I slammed the ice ball into! As I was hearing the conversation getting louder, I decided I had better move to a bigger bush, one that was taller than I and would cover my complete body from being seen. Then, just after I moved to the other bush, Postma and the undercover cop came right to where I had just been crouched down. The undercover cop had a flashlight and beamed it right at the place where I had been crouched down just minutes before. I overheard Postma pleading with the officer not to tell his parents and to let him go. In reality, the undercover cop was not about to let him go, making a trip afterwards to Postma's house and to my parents' house. My heartbeat was very quiet as I and my heart listened to the conversation. I was inwardly shocked that I had moved just in time to rid myself of facing the undercover cop whose car had been blasted by my ice ball. I could not see the cop's face. He did not flash the light towards my direction, so he knew not that I had been listening to their conversation.

They must have returned all the way to the other side to get into his car and take Reese to his parents' house, explaining what had transpired. To his house, it was only a block and a half. To our house, it was the other side of the block. I waited until the conversation died out and drifted in the wind and there was nothing heard. It was like coming out of a glass jar with protection all around it from the undercover cop who had sought out revenge on us. I was mesmerized as I made my way over to my friend's house, that of Jim Baker.

I knew that they would be going to my parents' house, so instead of returning home, I decided to stay at Jim Baker's house until late into the night. My friend Jim Baker had a pool table down in his basement, so we played pool there at times. This just so happened to be the best time to play pool and not get scolded by the undercover policemen that had visited our home. Robb soon came knocking on the door and probably had thought the same. My brother and I escaped the undercover cop, but my parents were not enthused about the news. We were both grounded, probably for a longer time than normal: a week.

Wrongcrowdhood

I had met some friends at school who were smokers. They liked to smoke cigarettes, skip school and walk up and down the street nearby the high school, Midland High. During lunch hours a few times, I walked with them and they offered me a cigarette without paying for it, so I started smoking cigarettes. And many teenagers also went to the local casinos to play video games. There, I had met a few people and a few girls, too.

I slowly got involved with the wrong school kids and crowd for a while. They invited me to experience parties, drugs, and alcohol. For me, drinking was not fun, though I did get drunk a few times. I smoked longer than I had experienced drinking alcohol because I did not like the taste of it, and I preferred being in charge of my own mind.

"Wine *is* a mocker, strong drink *is* raging: and whosoever is deceived thereby is not wise."[20]

Once, I had been offered to deal drugs. I was not the drug dealer type, but I thought it would just be small scale and give it a try for once. My quest for drug dealing started and ended probably the same day. Henry, an Asian man, helped me with the marijuana that I was offered to sell, to put it into a certain amount and told me how much I should sell it for. Then not long after, at the casino, there were some kids there who were looking for some marijuana. I told them that I had some, gave them the amount it was selling for, and talked with them while they were in the car. I was on the outside of the car talking with them through the open window. The car had been parked with the front of the car facing the casino. They took the marijuana in its casing, looked at it as though they were interested, and the driver started the car. I was not aware of their plans, but as the marijuana was in the car, the driver quickly put it into reverse and started back to leave me

---

[20] Prov. 20:1

71

without the payment. There was no car parked next to them, so as they were pulling back, I opened the passenger door. I yelled at him, "Give it back! "The boy in the passenger seat was shocked and surprised to find that I had opened the door and yelled at him, so he instinctively jumped back towards the driver. By that time, the driver had put it in drive and drove off as the door came shut again. That was the first and last attempt I made at dealing marijuana! It just took a turn towards being dangerous, and I was not in for it.

I had also met a man at the casino who was part of the National Guard. He seemed friendly enough, but he was quite deep into drugs and alcohol. The National Guard friend was a drinker who liked parties. He came to the casino once to invite me and my other two friends to a party in another town, Bay City, a thirty-minute drive at that time from Midland. At the time, I had been wearing contact lenses. The party was mostly for drinking, and the chauffeur, the National Guardsman, became plastered, insomuch that his walk was detected as a person who had downed too many!

As time progressed, I had explained to my two school friends and the National Guardsman that I needed to get home since I had to take out my contact lenses. Besides, I did not want to spend the night there anyhow. I had not touched alcohol, but the driver was the drunkest of all of us, and clearly could hardly walk a straight line! I had asked the man if I could drive home instead. He refused because he did not believe in allowing anyone to drive his car. At that, we were a bit worried, and I, knowing God, decided it best to pray and seek God in the car, asking for His protection. In fact, while we were driving down the road, swerving here and there, I told God that if He would get me out of that intense situation and get me home safe and in one piece, I would serve Him again. We arrived without any accident, God delivering us, so I did want to serve Him again.

At the same casino is where I had met a few younger and very pretty gals, and later, the one who would become my girlfriend. While we played cards, we also began playing footsie, the idea of placing one's foot upon the other person's foot of whom one likes. That, in itself, grew into a relationship and a liking for one another. We had sat down to play cards, usually with four people. Card playing at the casino is where I met not only my girlfriend but who would become my first wife. There were some things that were different with her: she had had a child already and was pregnant with another child. This is where it gets a little strange: The child that she had already was that of Alex, the boy I met in the Lutheran school who was my friend. Alex, of course, was no longer interested in the relationship with her, but he also had a friend, who happened to get the girl pregnant. He was interested in the relationship, probably even more so due to the pregnancy, his child in her womb; yet, her thoughts were, she was finished with him, too. Then, I came into the picture as a person whom she liked. I questioned whether I should accept her, as she had already had a kid and she had been pregnant and was going to give birth to a newborn from another. I was in a quandary as to what direction to take. However, I seemed to have a soft heart, and almost felt like the Lord, that I should not refuse. As I was a young teenager, I had drifted from the foundation that was laid up in me. It was during those days that I had picked up a habit of smoking cigarettes, doing some drugs, like marijuana and sometimes LSD, and going to parties drinking. As to the girl, I had just accepted her for who she was without any judgment towards her past, but do remember once, while sitting in my grandpa's truck that became our family's truck, because he had passed away, was I doing right by accepting this girl with this ordeal?

A teenager doesn't really know
How to make the right decisions
He's faced with decisions that will affect his future
He needs a lot of counsel

That counsel he may refuse
Make up his own mind
Live the life that he chooses
And later find the consequences

For me, counsel was not provided
Because counsel was not sought
I had not known how to seek counsel
I just had thought: It would all turn out all right.

No Parental Controlhood

Her family happened to be quite staunch Catholics. I had no knowledge, really, of the deep history of the Catholic beliefs at that age. The only thing I knew is that they were extremely different in their instructions from my upbringing. The girl wanted to live away from the control of her parents; yet she cherished any financial or food assistance they provided from time to time and, sometimes, at her petition.

The girlfriend, whom I shall name Betty, had a young daughter, whom I will call Carol. Carol's biological dad really did not see Carol. He was not in her life at all, so one could say, I kind of took over the role of daddy at an extremely young age. I was only seventeen years old at the time. I had no philosophy on how to raise children. I just assumed that one should be taking care of them the best one can. At the age of seventeen, I had a girlfriend who had a daughter from one who was my friend in grade school, the private Lutheran school. She was already pregnant from another person, and I was to take care of the child and the girlfriend both.

As is common to many in-laws, the relationship is always a bit tense. The son-in-law is always the outlaw. Because of their beliefs as staunch Catholics, that did not make it any rosier. That which tipped over the iceberg, one can say, is the fight for control of Carol. Grandma Dora, I will name her, was married to Grandpa Eddy. This family had three children living with them at the time, but they had all been adopted. Betty was an adopted girl into this family, so her biological dad and mom were nonexistent in her life, as she knew them not. One could also say, then, that her likes and dislikes, her mannerisms and her appearance were all completely different from the adoptive parents.

In retrospect, also, the religion that the parents had was not engrained in Betty, either. It did not seem to be a part of her life at all. For her, religion was nonexistent, also. She made no effort to be in any church, that is, until I turned over a new leaf, for my influence in her life was to turn her life around as well, later.

Yet there was Carol, the young girl who, in the eyes of Grandma, was a gem-like creature that did nothing wrong and who should receive no boundaries as to her conduct, either. That was one area, too, that made my inner being feel like I needed to plant my foot down. As long as I was going to become the leader of my own family, and Carol was going to be in it, I was going to rescue her from her Grandma Dora's control, though Grandma Dora did not control Carol. Rather, it was an unwritten, unspoken fight over who would gain the control over Carol. Nevertheless, something that probably all of us did not foresee is this fact: Carol was the one who wished control over her own self.

In-laws, outlaws
Fighting for control
Over the kids is the key
Grandparents want
All freedom without boundary
For their grandchildren

Grandma-in-law
Against son-in-law
Fighting for the right
To control the child
Certainly, there is a key point
A big disagreement will surface
The whole point is—control
Who is the one that calls the shots
Influences the others to follow their demands
And if not?

The gun[21] will be uploaded

---

[21] Mouth

For such as time as this
To manifest the presence
Of force since voluntary will
Does not suffice
Yet, then, something surfaces
All lose control
To the child who took it away

Yet the only thing that surfaced up to this time, before marriage, and up until marriage, would be the sealing of the seeds of war—seeds of that jealousy beginning to be planted. I knew they were deep within me being sprouted. Whether or not they were being planted in the in-laws, I could not tell, nor could I frankly discuss these matters, for then, that discussion would feel like a capitulation. I could tell, through this relationship, a war was on the horizon, even at my young age of seventeen. The armies were taking up their positions, observing their location, their strategies, and movement was, indeed, towards control. It was seen, and it had felt like a strangling grip that wished the person's death.

Betty also wished for me to live with her. She had gotten an apartment, somehow, and was living alone, but she had asked me to join her. I knew that I could not in any way consult with my parents, for they would reject it. As a teenage boy, nothing negative is accepted. Even though one knows in the back of his or her mind what one is doing is definitely not based on good conscience, I was not capable nor strong enough morally, one could say, to back down on the offer. However, in view of my parents' teachings and what was being requested, and knowing the rebellious years of teenagers, there seemed to be only one solution: run away! I would just leave without any counsel or any news about my plans.

She had, indeed, the same rebellious teenage years creeping upon her. She had depended much on her parents, but at the same time, she did not want to live with them nor follow their counsel or guidelines. Though their guidelines were not strenuous, the only problem that stuck in my head about them was the fact that they loved to manipulate a person to do as they wished rather than allow the person to have the freedom of choice. It may have been this that had caused Betty, at the time, to seek an apartment to live separately from her adoptive parents. Yet, in retrospect, she had had no job. To the contrary, the idea was to siphon off monies from the state by good taxpayers; though during those years, that does not impact the mind of the youth. What impacts their minds more is the overwhelming desire to become free without any responsibility. We did not realize that living in an apartment with monies from the state was in any way wrong. Since the government was going to provide monies from the taxpayers for us in our rebellion, because we wished not being in our parents' home and under their authority (though, in reality, we could do almost anything we wished, but that tad minute part that we wanted to get rid of, we were able to with government support).We were all gung-ho for that type of freedom, a libertarian freedom, if you will, without any restraint whatsoever, without borders, without anyone to tell us what to do. Our goal was to have total freedom from parental control, changing support monies for food and shelter from the parents to the state. Thus, one could say, our parents became the state.

Therefore, it was, essentially, replacing parental control or guidance to state control and guidance. Of course, with the state, it only minimally aided to the point that one has to, at times, even get parental assistance, too, to make ends meet. Then, there was the competition between the state and the parents for monies and support. The reality is delighting in the funds from the state, for that gave us opportunity to get out from under our parents' homes and authority, but since that does not suffice the appetite of the youth, nagging the parents for some extra funds is the true course of events. Thus, one could say, it goes from total parental control to state funding (and control?) with the so-called promise of freedom without responsibility, only because one lives on one's own.

Since the state provided funding, that meant that others in society who were taxpayers were paying for this escapade (thank you, Michigan, and the federal government), our not wishing to be living under the roof of our parents, she to hers and me to mine. Deep within, though, I kind of felt a tinge of disgust towards depending upon the state to provide any funding for my living. I preferred to make it on my own. Though, still, back then, I was only a teenager with a mind of my own to do as I pleased. Yet I noticed that my behavior had caused my mom to feel hurt inside. As a teenager, one may not really realize that our behavior affects the emotions of other people, especially those who are concerned for our welfare. Teenagers may act irreverently towards others, but they do not, in essence, understand that their behavior is actually causing others to feel emotional hurt. The teenager may seem aloof to that emotion.

Instead of explaining this to my parents, who were Christians and churchgoers, I just decided to leave without any explanation of where I was headed. It was an experience that my conscience was very much into bothering me about. The apartment rented was used even for parties, but I always went to bed at a decent hour, nonetheless, not caring for the extra hours of drinking. This apartment, by the way, as I understand, was rented out by a pastor at Pentecostal Temple. That pastor, Roger Barcus, had even asked the church to pray for the unruly people that he had rented the apartment to.

It was about a month afterwards that I had decided to return to my parents' home to explain to them about my whereabouts. My mother burst into tears upon my entrance and my coldness of heart by not explaining to her where I had been and where I had gone. To me, I was a bit shocked to see the tears come from her. It was unexpected. I did not think I meant that much or what I had done was all that wrong. My conscience did bother me now and then, and my mom's tears were that clincher that made living with this gal not exciting anymore. I preferred a heart at peace and a happy Mom, too. She had even mentioned that I did not have that much time left before I would enter the military anyhow, so it would be better to spend the time with them before leaving. I knew she was right, and I was wrong. At that moment, I decided it best to return at the end of the month. I had to explain to my girlfriend the situation, the feelings that Mom had felt, so it would be easier to leave.

Furthermore, what I had decided earlier about returning to God was on my mind, too. Thus, returning to my parents' home was a step in the right direction and one that would eventually stir me towards the pathway to God. My decision, then, was not only to return to my parents' home but also to begin my returning to serving God.

Mom and conscience worked together
To bring me back to my senses
Living in rebellion is
Not mechanically beneficial for the conscience
Neither is harming my parents' emotions
Or inviting the taxpayer to fund my escapade
Little did I know
All the harm that I had been causing
Leaving the home because I wanted on my own
To be with a girl
Without jobs to pay for rent or food
To have the taxpayer foot the bill
Is not conducive to teaching the community
And to live as such will bring about harm
And not the community we wish

High-schoolhood

In October 1983, I had signed up to join the Army for an entrance date of August 1st, 1984. I remember those great commercials on TV that looked so fascinating: "Be all you can be!" It looked so promising! The counselor at the high school had to discuss the plans of the youth with them. When we met for discussion, I had already had in my mind that I was going into the Army for life. Therefore, during that discussion of ours, everything she had to say was going in one ear and out the other. I noticed, though, as soon as I told her what my plans were, she did not try to convince me otherwise. She let it be. I did not like school at all like most people my age. Only few people loved it. The rest dreaded opening the school doors, walking down the hallway with a backpack on, carrying a load of books, and entering a classroom full of students who hated school. It was as though hate filled their appetite. How could the teachers even want to be a teacher with so many children who hated school and dreaded coming?

I can hardly imagine how the teachers felt preparing their time for teenagers who walked into the classroom with blank stares on their faces ready to leave at the sound of the bell and hating everything about school, the teachers, the hallways, the lockers, the principal, the rules, the books, especially the textbooks with all those new and strange terms in them. The only thing that might have made the day brighter for boys is the idea of girls attending. Everything else must have been drab, dreary, and unenlightening. How could a boy receive any great ideas when his mind is full of drudgery?

For the smokers in high school, they raced upon the sounding of the bell, to the first door they could get out. The high school did not allow anyone to smoke inside the building, but still, at that time of history, they still allowed the teenagers to smoke just outside the building, whichever doors they could open and get outside. One thing sticks in my memory, though: how could a high school permit underage kids to smoke cigarettes on school grounds? It did not make sense to me. But I was never involved in smoking outside the building with those crowds. I noticed, of course, the smokers were the last ones to come into the classroom, and sometimes, they entered their class a bit late, sometimes even behind the late teachers.

I remember some of the high school teachers' faces. I remember the biology instructor who had asked us to write down our thoughts of evolution. My friend, Chris, who sat next to me had told me that he was going to write in favor of evolution, not because he really believed it but because he could possibly use the book or explain it better. I thought about doing the same, but my conscience did not allow me to lie to the biology teacher. The biology teacher, no doubt, had already made up his mind, but I was going to write the truth to him on the paper so that he might see not all school-aged children who come to public schools believe in the nonsense of evolution. I disagreed with my friend and classmate, Chris, whom I even played baseball with, for writing something to the biology teacher that he himself did not believe. Instead, I thought the biology teacher should know the truth from my heart, instead of evolution from a mixture of a monkey's heart to his. Mine just did not have the monkey in it at the time. My conscience did not want monkey blood flowing through it, so I followed my conscience that time. My friend next to me, however, thought differently. Maybe, he did have some mixture of monkey heart.

The evolutionists hail Darwin
For finding what they thought was truth
A monkey's heart for everyone
And a monkey's brain to boot

That might have been
What caused my psychosis
The mad cow mooed not so
It was his blood that did it

Truthfully, though, I am
Just monkeying around
For I had found it stated,
"So God created man in his own image,
in the image of God created he him;
male and female created he them,"
In Genesis 1:27, you see

In reading that I found
That I had not a monkey's brain at all
I was more intelligent,
For the Creator decided
I would get more
Than a monkey's brain could hold

The cow mooed again and said
That he had tried to deposit in me
His image, you see
To make me go insane

However, the doctor disagreed
At least, I think he did
For he had more intelligence
Than a monkey did

And the cow couldn't
Give his brain away to me
For I had a more intelligent one, you see
From the Creator who let me know
By the word of God, you see

I do not remember any of the high school teacher names. Wait, I take that
back. There was one teacher I do remember. He was the coolest teacher. His

name was Carter, an African American PE teacher. He got by with not giving difficult exams and had everybody relax, exercise, or play sports. That job seemed easy. Really, he probably had the best job in the high school. And the reaction from the students he taught was not one of trying to put their heads into a book to cram it into their minds, but he had dealt with students who were eager to do some kind of sport to exercise their will with a game or two. It made the students feel better inwardly, to vent their frustrations on a ball, whacking it back and forth or deliberately or accidently hitting another student on the court. Furthermore, everyone thought the physical education teacher was the best. He fit into the category of jocks in the school. He could have been considered not as a jock but as the jock of the school. He was disconnected with the sports teams, at least in my perception, because I attended not to sports after school hours. To me, he appeared to be a regular schoolteacher and not one who coached any sports after hours. Those teachers who coached sports after school were different.

The two others, I now recall too, Jozwiak and Wilczek, were coaches, though they had had their regular subjects to instruct. As far as I am concerned, those two instructors and coaches were not precisely classified as jocks, per se, but their dedication for school was to work with the class of students named jocks. They were probably hinted at by the principal to keep the jocks away from the partiers. That is, at certain times, there may have been inspection as to their mental status, their breath, their drug levels. If at any time the coaches felt that the jocks were moving into the status of another category such as the partiers, they would conduct some tests of alcohol or drug levels and make it their duty to penalize the students for having placed themselves into the wrong group at school.

Besides this task, their other task was to vent their frustrations out on the students during public events and to do so legally, looking as though they were working hard. Inside, however, they were glad to have the opportunity to yell at the top of their lungs at any jock who was acting a little less than a jock. Their anger and frustration could be played out in front of the public view instead of only the classroom. They really could not show this type of anger at the students in the classroom, but during sports competition, slight mistakes and their bitter feelings could easily vent themselves in front of all watching and listening ears, making their hearts jump for joy that they were able to un-clog their lungs and raise their voices to the highest pitch of frustration at stu-dents who may have fumbled. Though one would consider each team or even people to have bad days, the jocks were not allowed to have bad days. Bad days did not exist in their mental vocabulary. The bad days for the jocks were the days the coach used his strength within his lungs to pour out his frustration from the day's setback of peering at haters in school.

This other instructor, named Gary Jozwiak, in turning to pages of histori-cal accounts, state that he was an excellent coach.[22] The only thing I remember about him is that he coached football in high school, Midland High School, the high school named after the city. The other competitive high school was named after Dow, the biggest employer in Midland. Somehow, the biggest employer got to compete against the city. Instructor and Coach Jozwiak looked the part of a football coach, though, really, because he did look stern. When our family went to the football games, we all rooted for the city. So, we were, also rooting for Coach Jozwiak, but in retrospect, I do not re-member if he was one of my instructors, too, and I cannot even recall the subject if he was.

Terry Wilczek, on the other hand, was the English teacher (and another football coach if I am right) I remember vaguely. I remember him because, as I recall, he had the biggest mustache in school. It was one of those macho mus-taches that forced students to pay attention. He was stern, too, in his looks, but I am not sure where his heart was. It may have been more towards his mus-tache. These two were the coaches of football, so maybe that is why I re-member them more, because they had it right: football was culturally American, and soccer was not. Mr. Wilczek taught English, but my success in English was scant at that time. It was not his fault, really. If I were to fault any-thing, it would be his mustache.

I also do not know how some could actually stay after school hours to play any types of sports. Well, that was for the jocks of the school. For me, any school life was a drudgery, but I would classify myself at that time as having

---

[22] Chris Stevens. "Jozwiak Still Involved with the Game He Loves." Midland Daily News. March 24, 2016. https://www.ourmidland.com/news/article/Jozwiak-still-involved-with-the-game-he-loves-7024892.php.

tested the boundaries of a jock and a partier, but as a brain, I think not. The true classification might even be a homebody, but my mom would disagree with that. Being around any other classmates from school would remind me of classes, so I preferred not to stay at all. As soon as the bell for the last class sounded, I walked home, thankful another dreaded day of school had ended. And as far as the textbooks were concerned, though I might have had homework, they might have been opened, and I might have done my homework, but I had no joy in doing any of it. Further, it was the last thing for the day. In addition, my heart was about as far away from the learning, the reading, the textbooks, and the homework as much as the farthest star is from this planet Earth, and who knows what name that star has? The textbook did not have the answer, and nobody did, either. There was only one that had the answer, the one who made it possible for us to read the Bible, God Himself.

As soon as one walked out of the school doors, hate could not continue with the students' hearts: they all left it for the next morning upon entrance.

In summary, then, I have concluded there were three types of people who attended high school: the brains, the jocks, and the partiers. I did not fit in any of these categories. I was a misfit. The jocks were the ones who attended and entered the sports events. Some of the partiers came to the football match, but it was probably only to meet together with the other partiers and head off to drink or party here or there, giving their parents the idea that they'd be at the game. And those who had the brains were only at home studying to make their minds expand.

And just like that, high school was completed…
Three categories of high school students:
The brains, the jocks, and the partiers
These categories molded the students To attend to their class

The others were misfits
Stared at by all three categories Teachers paying attention only
To students in each of these categories Selecting their preference inwardly

To have more conversations with the group they liked

In reality, though, the brains were the ones
Who held the conversations with the teachers most
The partiers hid behind a cloud of smoke
The jocks thought about their games and practice
And I was out of touch with all three groups
Even the teachers did not reach out
To one as silent as a fish

Army Lifehood

I went to basic training in Fort Knox, Kentucky. The first day we had arrived, our duty was to get our uniforms and receive all the basic equipment necessary for training. That day lasted on into the next day without having any sleep. That was a nightmare without a dream. I had never stayed up all night long, even though I had gone to a few parties in my life. I had always made it a habit to get in bed and sleep, for the night was necessary to get sleep for the brain to think properly.

The shock of that and the fact of the drill sergeants shouting out commands and belittling us who were to be mentally trained as well put a reverse into my planning. I wanted out of the military that day, the first day. I concocted a scheme of trying to leave basic training, but it was never realized. Instead, I stayed the entire three years, but I did get out without reenlisting or extending.

It was during those hardship days of training and receiving the biggest belittling of our lives that had given me an incentive to search the scriptures, read, and get acquainted more thoroughly with God as a comfort for my soul. During our break times, that was probably the only book I had read. Others would talk. I would read the Bible.

During those readings, I came to the conclusion that I needed to get baptized. Of course, I had not recalled being baptized as an infant, and nobody had mentioned it to me, either. Thus, I began writing a letter to my former home church in Midland regarding baptism to the youth pastor. He had stated that even though they were in a building program, no one else during that cold season of winter would be on the list for baptism. And they would have to use another church's baptismal tank to baptize me; therefore, it would be best for me to continue on in prayer and ask God to provide it another time.

The letter was hard to grasp for me at basic training while I had been look-ing for encouragement and an answer from God; yet God had other plans in mind somewhere else.

At the end of basic training, all of us got into a formation and received our orders. My orders must have been ordered of the Lord, for where I was headed, God had His plans laid out for me. I had received orders for Fort Polk, Louisiana, one of the Bible Belt states and a nearby town of Leesville, LA, with only a population of fourteen thousand people, but with five UPCI churches to attend.

First Duty Stationhood

Of course, I knew nothing of this duty station, so I was in anticipation. It would be the first time traveling to a far distant city away from home, never doing so before and at such a young age and a great responsibility ahead of me. I was only of the age of 18 years with a wife and her daughter with the requirements of finding a home in Fort Polk, LA, or the adjoining city of Leesville, LA. Further, I did not go first and seek out a place; rather, we all went at the same time in different vehicles not knowing whether we would find a place right away. Yet, as a young teenager, and one who was interested in serving God, I knew that God would provide, and I had faith that He would do so!

Our first car, a white Honda Civic, had been given to us by my in-laws, for our wedding gift. Our wedding was hosted at the church I had attended as a teenager, and the date was set for between basic training and the date I needed to be present at my first duty station. That white Honda was the only car that we owned at the time, and I probably could not have purchased any other due to financial constraints, but I also had a Suzuki 250cc motorcycle.

The blue Suzuki 250cc was placed in the U-Haul, plus the very formal dining table given to us by my grandparents for our wedding gift also with the conception in Grandma's mind—though no one else's—that we as a couple would never give it away or sell it, but we would keep it on hand for our entire lives. The problem with that was, we were in the military, though, and the military frequently sent us soldiers to various locations abroad. My grandparents were not from military families, and maybe they had not known about that fact, because, once we had to get rid of it and not take it with us, Grandma was terribly upset. Albeit, what was I to do but to carry it all the way to Germany and back, paying for the shipping costs on my low salary? Had she known that we would give it away later, she would never have given it to us.

Yet military personnel frequently change their address, even move overseas, and some of the goods are really only a burden rather than a blessing, unfortunately. To this day, I feel saddened by the expectation of Grandma upon us that I could not fulfill.

Back then, the way to find oneself across the USA from the north, in Michigan, to the furthest state south (in that direction), Louisiana, was to buy a book of maps with all the highways of the states. Moreover, one of us had to drive the U-Haul truck and the other the Honda Civic. In addition, there were no cell phones back then. Thus, there was no way to communicate between vehicles, and the only way to stick together was to drive together without losing one another.

Further, I recall no credit cards in my pocket, either. The money I had saved up was that of my paychecks from basic training for moving from Michigan all the way to Louisiana. I must have had a bank account at Chemical Bank in Midland but, out of necessity, had to transfer my funds to another bank in Louisiana, setting up another bank account there. Thus, it was a matter of carrying the cash all the way from Midland to Louisiana in my billfold. I am not sure how much money my former wife had at the time she had been driving the Honda Civic, but when we got to a place where we almost got separated, I had thought about it more sincerely. Luckily, we were not separated, and all went very well all the way down to Louisiana.

We must have stayed in a hotel for a few nights in Leesville while I searched the newspaper for apartments or houses for rent. There was no other way to search for places to live due to the time frame that I had, and I was not about to go there, find a place, and send for them. Instead, we just planned to move there and pray for a place to become available.

God had His plan for us on the way down there. It was urgent that we find a rental right away. In our search for houses, one was available just down the street from the UPCI church that we would attend, starting near Christmas time. Little did I know that the owner who would rent to us would be assisting the same church I would later find to attend and get baptized in. The landlord did not look for any references as they might today. I remember nothing about extending any list of references for any reason at all. Instead, I was interested in renting the home; he was interested in renting the home to us, so we made a deal. No background checks were necessary; besides, what background would I have had at the early age of eighteen anyhow?

The newspaper was for me the only way to find houses or apartments. This rented home that had been published in the newspaper was a one-bedroom small house with the landlord, unbeknownst to me, who had attended the United Pentecostal Church down the street. Thus, before I came into the UPCI, I had already had two landlords that were from the UPCI, the first two landlords and the first two homes, also, without knowing that they were both from the same organization!

Since it was furnished, also, there was no need to buy any furnishings. All was provided. In any case, since the military gave orders frequently to soldiers, it would have been quite a hassle to purchase furnishings, then try and get rid of them. Thus, a furnished house just made it all that much less hassle when the time had come to leave Leesville.

That church had a sign out front that Sunday school was at 10:00 a.m. and an evening service was scheduled for 7:00 p.m., I believe. The sign for Sunday school discouraged me from attending because I had thought I just wanted to attend service and not Sunday school. I was of the opinion that Sunday school was for kids, and if it were for adults, I did not want people to investigate about my life during Sunday school. It would be easier just to go to the main sanctuary and fit behind the crowd.

Because of that fact, I preferred other churches to visit first: the Baptists and the Assembly of God, too, were the extent of my search. However, these suited not my taste. Then, come one Sunday morning, I had overslept. Therefore, in taking into consideration the availability in the evening that the United Pentecostal Church down the road had an evening service, I decided to attend to fit in my Sunday church going. It was also during the Christmas season, so it was doubly important.

They were delighted to see a walk-in without anyone else's invitation, as though a stranger walking in was a delight to everyone: someone new had come in the door. That evening, they played in a Christmas drama. The pastor, at some moments, was playing the steel guitar, the only thing that I recall about the drama. Of course, I had never seen a church pastor on a steel guitar in my entire short church life, but he played it so well and was expert at it. One of the things, besides many others, of that which I remember of who became my spiritual father, Pastor Thomas Gibson, was that even in his refusal of certain things, he said it in such a way that when one received the refusal, it was full of apologizing or a sense that he was humble in his way of explaining it. That made me feel comfortable, even though he did refuse some requests of certain things.

That Christmas drama night, we were both invited to come back for the Wednesday evening service. Of course, that was on my list for things to do right away. The services were very appreciated, because of the people's worship. It seemed to flow with songs and specials, hands being raised, clapping and sometimes a shout was heard. Though not professionals in the least, their heartfelt worship was exuberant in their appearance and praise. The praise service was of my approval. That had passed my inspection. Moreover, what intrigued me was the fact that the people were country folk, pleasant, down-to-earth, friendly, and extremely courteous. The preaching was the next step to get approval.

Gospelhood

Pastor Gibson, I later found out and observed, was of the stricter sort. Betty had noticed something I did not: All the ladies were in skirts or dresses, and she was the only one with different apparel on. After the wonderful singing, special songs, and the playing of the steel guitar by the pastor, the pastor moved to the podium for the message from God. Pastor Gibson was of the age of fifty-two, so he was not a young man; further, he had been ministering for some time and knew how to deal with newcomers like us.

He had opened his Bible to Acts 2:38, announcing to the congregation of that scripture. Personally, in my Bible reading, I had not noticed that particular verse of scripture nor did it come out in any special way before his message. Yet he did not hide what he intended to have the congregation know (but, in truth, they had already known what he was preaching about and had heard it before—we were the ones who had not heard it the way he was emphasizing it before).

"Then Peter said unto them, Repent, and be baptized every one of you in the name of Jesus Christ for the remission of sins, and ye shall receive the gift of the Holy Ghost."[23]

For him and for Oneness Apostolic brothers and sisters, that was the scripture that held what to do for the sinner, so it was important for the sinners to know what to do if they wanted their lives to be changed by God. He was not shy to preach that truth, even when a newcomer had entered the door of the church. Further, he was not apologetic of any truth that he had preached and which, he believed, came from God. And he knew also that many newcomers would not know this scripture considering how they and he had understood it. What was also very intriguing, though, was the fact that he was preaching

---

[23] Acts 2:38

about baptism too, since I had been looking for this, but his focus was on the reception of the Holy Spirit.

What I had been taught growing up was the following: The reception of the Holy Spirit was an extra gift for the church just like other gifts written about by the Apostle Paul in Corinthians. These other gifts include the gift of tongues, interpretation of tongues, healing, the word of knowledge, prophecy, and so on. Thus, these gifts were not mandatory to receive, but they are gifts that if one were to receive them, one would be able to bless others with them and be blessed with those gifts, too.

However, he was not preaching that the gift of the Holy Spirit was an extra gift, but he was preaching that it was necessary for my salvation! In retrospect, this was, to me, an extremely serious moment—the moment that one receives the gospel message and the response included in that hearing. It is this moment that Jesus, the church, and angels work together to provide for sinners an opportunity and a choice to believe and obey the message. It is at that moment that one's response could determine one's eternity. The enemy would always like to try to make this moment look not that important and the message of no value; however, the reality is, this is a defining moment in the life of souls. That moment is being recorded in heaven, as is every other moment, but the one moment that Jesus had shed His blood for, to have people receive the gospel message! The seed was being planted, the seed of the kingdom of God! This minister seemed to be urging me to believe this message as a spiritual need for eternal life.

Held in the balance of an eternal decision
The weight of that moment
Has been paid for by the coming of Jesus
Shedding His blood for all of humanity
Hanging on a cross due to my sin and shame

The preparation of that moment
Has been made by Jesus Christ
Angels, ministers, and saints alike

Making it the precise moment
That a decision must be made
From the candidate in question
What will the person decide?

This decision made
Will affect one's eternity
Refusal could lead the one to a desperate eternity
The acceptance to a bright light of heaven's gates
It is the message of the gospel that was provided
By the One who created us
And by the One who came and lived among us
And suffered for our sins and shame
It behooves men to incline an ear
To open their heart's door
And let the King of glory come in!

He did step on my toes of my former church instruction, and he knew that that would be the case, but he did not change the message to dilute it in any way. He preached it thoroughly, clearly, and in respect to God, who had made the sacrifice for the message to be brought to me on that lovely day.

What he preached was this: That if one did not follow the guidelines laid out in Acts 2:38, in regard to repenting, being baptized in Jesus's name and receiving the Holy Spirit, they were, in fact, not headed to heaven. He proclaimed that they were on their way to hell.

Even though he did preach it that way, I felt no condemnation at that point. I often wonder why I would not feel condemnation. The response to that is clearly I was not rejecting the message at all. I appreciated the message that the preacher had provided as the vessel used of God at that moment for His glory and work. It was exactly what the Lord had ordered, nothing less. To me, I wished baptism. Of course, at the time of the baptism, I had not known that there were churches that baptized differently. Perhaps there are many people who also face baptism and do not know that some churches across the world baptize in different ways. All that I had known was the fact that I was desperately seeking baptism and had been seeking it for some time already.

Thus, I must be frank and honest in my explanation here about baptism: From the churches that I had attended in my upbringing, they had baptized people saying, "In the name of the Father, and of the Son, and of the Holy Ghost. "In the Lutheran faith, such as I had received as a baby, I was sprinkled with water, "In the name of the Father, and of the Son, and of the Holy Spirit." I remember my mother's baptism at the Assembly of God church. They baptize in immersion in the name "of the Father, and of the Son, and of the Holy Ghost. "However, this preacher believed in the baptism in the name of Jesus Christ and did not repeat the words "in the name of the Father, and of the Son, and of the Holy Spirit. "Instead, he pronounced the name of Jesus Christ over me in my baptism, and it was done completely underwater, that is, in immersion. Thus, in retrospect, I could say this, that God answered my prayers better than I had expected, for He led me to the true way to get baptized, in His name!

Regarding receiving the Holy Spirit, I just thought he had a different viewpoint. And when the invitation to come to the altar was given, there were some ladies who came to where I was seated. They did not grab my hand and haul me to the altar, but they came discretely and reverently, asking if I would like to go to the altar and pray there. I was in no mood to resist. I really liked the worship and the preaching, frankly speaking. And for them to come to the place where I had been sitting, asking me to come to the altar and pray, I was in an agreeable mood. In fact, in retrospect, that might have been the only way they could have gotten me to the altar because I probably would not have gone. The only way for the paralyzed man to get to Jesus Christ was to have him carried to Jesus! This illustration fits perfectly for the sinners that need Jesus. Perhaps they need some extra encouragement and some people who will ask them to come to the altar and pray. I went willingly upon their petition.

A call to come and pray
Had been given
It was from the preacher
And the saints stood and waited

Many hear the call from the preacher
Yet few may actually step out
It takes an extra few
To advise them on their journey
To come out of their pew
And walk down the aisle
To find Christ at the altar

Some may just be too shy to reach out
They know little of the importance of praying
And praying at an altar, they may not have known
But it is the spark that drives people to see the truth
And receive the Holy Spirit

The invitation may have been given by the pastor, and the ladies were there to do their job, too. They must have known that people may need an extra hand, a personal invitation rather than just a public invitation by the pastor. Surely, there are those that will come if they get an invitation by the pastor; however, there are those who may not be ready or willing to go up to the altar if it is an invitation for all, especially when that person might be the only one that will go or the others in the congregation only expect the guests to come to the altar. The personal invitation was much more intriguing, a first of its kind for me, and it did its work.

The ladies at the altar were more dynamic than the men were, as is common. Betty had gone to the altar too. As soon as she had gotten to the area of the altar, I remember clearly she had fallen back, speaking in tongues. One of the ladies must have been behind her when she had fallen, no doubt, under the power of God. Her tongue was loosed, and she just kept speaking in other tongues.

Meanwhile, for me, I was led to pray at the altar, but I had found myself praying on the lady's side quite alone. The men were on the other side of the altar area, probably waiting for me to realize that I needed to move over with them. No one had said anything to me regarding the idea that I needed to pray on the side where the men were. It just did not dawn upon me that I had been praying on the side where the ladies were having a victory shout. I kind of liked the victory shout! The men seemed quieter. Nevertheless, in my prayer and in my contemplation, at the moment, I had had no hard feelings against the pastor in any way for his dynamic, powerful, and straightforward message. The message did not feel like it was condemning to me at all. I took it to heart, but I did say, upon kneeling at the altar and analyzing what he had said, that I prayed something like this: "God, you know my heart, and you know what he had preached, that it was necessary to have the Holy Spirit, but you know that I believe that it is an extra gift and not necessary." Of course, I did not have any scriptures available to point to in order to share my ideas with the Lord, but that is how I had been instructed, and that is how I felt at that moment.

Nevertheless, the question came up of whether I wanted to get baptized. I had not been instructed in any way with them except for that one sole message from the pastor regarding baptism in Jesus's name. However, I had already been ready and was all for it! I agreed immediately, but my former wife had said she needed to learn about it first. Thus, it took her a couple of weeks, but finally, on December 19th, 1984, both of us were baptized in the name of Jesus Christ!

They had a tank in the back, behind the platform area. It was heated up for us, but there were some conditions that the pastor had mentioned first. He did not want to baptize my former wife in pants, so she had to get a skirt on first. Secondly, he told me to take off my rings. When we were finally ready, the pastor prayed and baptized Betty and I in the name of Jesus Christ. When I came up out of the water, I had felt clean, purely clean in my soul, not understanding why at the moment. Later, upon instruction, I began realizing the reason for the cleanliness feeling. The cleanliness I had felt was from the inside, but I had no knowledge of why, really from that first moment. I had just noticed that I had felt really clean on the inside.

The next step of their methods for winning people and assisting in others being grounded in the truth was that one of the same ladies who had invited me to come to the altar invited me for a Search for Truth Bible study at our home. Betty and I believed we needed to have a home Bible study and readily agreed. There were several lessons taught, and the nice middle-aged lady came to our home regularly. That was something that I was so longing for and looking forward to each time! In fact, even when she had ended the entire Search for Truth Bible study lessons, I was intently desiring even more! Yet it was during these studies that she pointed out to me some of their beliefs, such as the word "Trinity" not found in the Bible. And when we had come to that topic of who Jesus is, the revelation of who He is came to me! I had found who He is! She had said that Jesus is God, the only God, the one true God! The teaching was concerning Jesus's humanity and divinity! It made clear sense to me! I had always agreed that in heaven, one would see only one sitting on the throne!

Hunger and thirst for the word of God
Had entered my being
With home Bible studies came
The desire to know more
The preaching of the word at church
Held great prominence
But it was enhanced by the lady
Who made her way to our door
Teaching Bible studies to us
On a weekly basis

The foundation was laid
Of the true gospel message
The revelation of the Oneness of God
Was made plain in those Bible studies
A tribute should be made
To Darlene who came willingly to teach
And share God's beautiful word with us!

Contemplationhood

That particular night on December 19th, 1984, my former wife and I headed home, and since I had not yet received the Holy Spirit, that was on my mind. Certainly, I was interested in everything that Darlene from church had ministered to us in the study of the Bible. I was very hungry for all of it. One thing I had begun contemplating was their concept of the necessity of the reception of the Holy Spirit.

The longer I continued to attend that local congregation, though, the more that message from the pastor reverberated in my thoughts. The contemplation of his message: if I do not have the Holy Spirit, I would be lost and go to hell! That was sincerely a strong message! I had never, ever heard it in such a way. I had only heard that the reception of the Holy Spirit was an extra gift. Yet the more I contemplated about his message, the more I began worrying that if he was right, and I was wrong, I was lost! Therefore, I not only contemplated about it, but Betty and I must have come to an agreement on that on the night of December 19th, 1984, right after baptism, she could help me in praying for the Holy Spirit. She had only received it recently, and I had not seen anyone else receive the Holy Spirit, either. The night that she had received the Holy Spirit, I was up praying at the altar with my head on the platform, so I did not actually observe the moment she had received the Holy Spirit, but I did witness the fact that she had been speaking in other tongues after I turned and sat down. The ladies had placed a microphone up to her mouth so that all in the congregation could hear her speaking in other tongues. I had heard it, too. As for me, no one seemed to be edging me on to pray. No one at that time had laid their hands on me to pray for me, either. All eyes, instead, were on Betty and what had happened to her.

But in the thought of the reception of the Holy Spirit for me, then, the only instruction that we had to receiving the Holy Spirit was that which the ladies had instructed Betty on that night that she had received the Holy Spirit. They were of the influence that praising God should be with a loud voice; for example, to keep repeating the word "Hallelujah" again and again in praise would allow God's presence to come, and one would feel a heaviness upon the tongue as though it was moving to speak other words or move in ways that were different from one's own language. The instruction went as follows: Once one feels that heaviness upon the tongue, that is the Spirit wanting to take control and start moving the tongue with a new language, not of one's own mother tongue or any learned language. One should somehow allow God's Spirit to move the tongue. It is like a partnered speech between the Spirit and the person. The person must allow one's own tongue to move as God directs.

We were in bed, and it felt like it was time for prayer to receive the Holy Spirit right then and there. The difference between praying at home and praying at the altar in the church was, since I was new, a matter of comfort. I had, obviously, felt more at ease praying without hindrance in my own home, whereas praying at the altar at church, one needed to heed time. When the others were slowing down in their prayers, it signaled I should, too. However, in my home, I was the one who was going to be putting all the effort in, and there would be no disturbances, no thoughts of what others might think of me, no discouragement if some others were to stop praying with me, either. I was only with Betty, so I could pray easily until I received the Holy Spirit. And that one night, I was determined I was going to pray until I received it!

Thus, faced with that thought--if I had not received the Holy Spirit with the evidence of speaking in other tongues, I was lost--I made up my mind to pray until I received the Holy Spirit! I did not want to wake up in hell. I wanted to go to heaven! Therefore, with the threat of going to hell in mind, I began praying more in earnestness, getting sincerely desperate. It really did not take that long, though, and I started speaking in other tongues as the Spirit gave me the utterance just like it was recorded in Acts 2. Joyful was I about it, because then I was no longer hanging in the balance.

Of course, news of me receiving the Holy Spirit had been announced to the pastor. Betty spread the news quickly among the congregation members. In the next service, then, Pastor Thomas Gibson asked me to stand and testify of that reception of the Holy Spirit to the congregation. I kind of thought he might ask because Betty had been asked, too, to testify when she had received the Holy Spirit. I stood and expressed that it was true. I had received the Holy Spirit, speaking in other tongues.

Faced with the threat of hell
I had made my decision
I wanted no part of it

With the gift of the Holy Spirit
I was all for it
I wanted what God had provided for me

Even though not in a church service
The prayer was made
The praise was going up
For the One who made it possible
To receive the Spirit anywhere

In a church service
I would be shier
I may have thoughts of people watching me
But at home, I was more comfortable

In the church service
People might stop praying
The pastor might conclude the service
But I was determined
I needed the Holy Spirit
I was going to pray until my answer came

I had all night, and I did not care
How long it took for me to receive it
However, God blessed, and it took no time
And soon I was speaking in another language!

Joyfulhood

One of the decisions I had to make was regarding going to church and not allowing myself to be distracted by other things, especially when church service was scheduled on Sunday mornings, evenings, and during the week. One of the things that could have been a problem was the movies that were showing on the nights that church service was scheduled. It just so happened that HBO had come out, and it was the first time in my life that I could get HBO, watch the programs that I desired, and not have anyone else direct me otherwise, change the channel, or even have Mom say, "What junk are you watching?"

Thus, I remember flipping through the pamphlet of the schedule of shows with a picture of the movie, the names, and viewing times. It just so happened that the movies that were more intriguing for me were on the nights that the services at the church were scheduled. Secondly, but I am not certain as to the timing, the pastor would preach against TV. I remember not the first time that I had heard him preach against it and whether it was during those days of our recent move to the church or not. In any case, Betty and I had only stayed in Louisiana for a period of eleven months; therefore, he must have spoken about it enough to make an influence in our lives. In fact, once leaving that church congregation and Pastor Thomas Gibson, even though I was among UPCI churches afterwards too, I had never heard anyone during those days and in the services preach so hard against TV, even to this day! It must have been God's way to use Him to put God's desire that TV is not for the fervent Christian! The movies were the most tempting because they were scheduled to conflict with the church services, and if anyone understands Pentecostal services, the Sunday evening services were usually the ones that people worshipped the Lord with more gusto and the presence of God flowed and touched people more. And the HBO movies, as everyone knows, were, at that time, without any commercials, and it was the first time that movies were shown in the home, almost like one was at the movie theater.

Yet even though the temptation had come to drop the service for movie viewing, I did not take that route. Instead, I held on to attending every service. With that decision, the Lord must have made my appointment to become blessed by Him in a profound way since it was a major decision to neglect movie viewing for church attendance. Moreover, it must not have been too long after hearing that the TV was not a good influence to have in one's home, I decided to part ways with it.

This decision must have actually paved the way for something else that I remember so vividly and that that experience was one of the most tremendous experiences I've ever had with God. One time after the preaching from Pastor Gibson, the people were up at the altar, men on one side, women on the other, and I was there praying and seeking God. Any time a person was at the altar praying, it was that person the others targeted and prayed for with their hands on their shoulders.

Most of the time, they wished for people to stand and lift their hands in worship to reach the victory! I had no qualms with that, because kneeling was quite hard to do for any length of time and keeping one's hands raised to get a blessing from God was easier. To stand with arms lifted only put the thought into one's mind that others might be watching, and if for any length of time, the arms might get tired. This time, though, that did not bother me. In fact, I had a thought that entered my mind: I should continue praying and not give up.

I listened to the advice of that still small voice and continued praying and seeking God. The men were gathered around me praying with their hands placed on my shoulders. It might have been between five and ten minutes when suddenly, coming seemingly out of nowhere, what hit me was only explainable later: the power of God moved through me to have me dance around the altar. In other words, it was not just God taking control of the tongue, but it was, in fact, God taking control of my entire body! It was like going into unconsciousness, God's Spirit overwhelming me, insomuch that what hit me was like a flame of fire that consumed every portion of my body! I began dancing around the altar area with, I suppose, my eyes closed. This dancing must have taken place a minute or so, and I remember vividly falling down to my knees full of the fire of God, exhausted completely! In fact, it was so powerful that it was as though He had taken complete control of my entire body. The fire of God was felt so strongly that I was totally overwhelmed. I had never experienced such a dramatic experience from God before! That experience also woke me up much more to the things of the Spirit of God! It was like a lightning bolt from heaven striking me from within, getting rid of any desire that did not please God! That experience made my day, and my spiritual life from then on felt like it was on cloud nine. I was so totally impressed by that experience that it kept me and helped me through many difficult and hard struggles in every area of my life.

Faced with a temptation of the world before my eyes
HBO was a lure
Church service for many was a bore
But there seemed to be a lore
With Oneness Pentecostalism

Throwing out the TV
Paved the way for God
To bless me with a profound experience with Him
That dancing almost unconsciously in His presence
Took all the desire of the world away

It was easy to see from then on
What a difference God had done
I was no longer won by the world
Instead I made Jesus the center of my world
I gave to Jesus my eyes
He gave me more than I imagined
He put the desire in my soul
Where the light of the body is the eye
For Himself to be strictly God
Him and no one else!

Strictly Fatherhood

My spiritual father, Thomas Gibson was his name, appeared not to have a strict line when he talked. When he talked with a person, he was very respectful, and he had an exceptionally fine way of apologizing for having to say no for something that he could not do. When he preached, his preaching was with power! He did preach against saints watching or having TVs in their homes. One of the scriptures that he had preached from, and one of the messages that I had tape recorded and listened to afterwards, was from the text of Psalm 101.

"I will behave myself wisely in a perfect way. O when wilt thou come unto me? I will walk within my house with a perfect heart. ³ I will set no wicked thing before mine eyes: I hate the work of them that turn aside; it shall not cleave to me.⁴ A froward heart shall depart from me: I will not know a wicked person.⁵ Whoso privily slandereth his neighbour, him will I cut off: him that hath an high look and a proud heart will not I suffer.⁶ Mine eyes shall be upon the faithful of the land, that they may dwell with me: he that walketh in a perfect way, he shall serve me.⁷ He that worketh deceit shall not dwell within my house: he that telleth lies shall not tarry in my sight.⁸ I will early destroy all the wicked of the land; that I may cut off all wicked doers from the city of the LORD."²⁴

It took me some time to accept his viewpoint that I should not have a TV nor even view movies or programs on TV. One of the things that people get from the TV is an abundance of information. However, today, information spreads by the Internet also, and the Internet is useful to provide the information that one wants rather than being fed by the TV that may provide information that one does not wish to receive. The idea is the power of control over one's own mind versus what may be slipped into the mind by the producers of movies without much moral control.

---

²⁴ Ps. 101:2–8

Thus, I accepted the fact of not having a TV. And when I began preaching, I also preached the same as he did: I believed the same as Acts 2:38 and did not believe that saints should have TV in their homes, either, for the purpose of holiness.

In fact, in reading the UPCI guidelines for holiness, it states the following:

"We wholeheartedly disapprove of our people indulging in any activities which are not conducive to good Christianity and godly living, such as theaters, dances, mixed bathing or swimming, women cutting their hair, make-up, any apparel that immodestly exposes the body, all worldly sports and amusements, and unwholesome radio programs and music. Furthermore, because of the display of all these evils on television, we disapprove of any of our people having television sets in their homes. We admonish all of our people to refrain from any of these practices in the interest of spiritual progress and the soon coming of the Lord for His church."[25]

Taking the counsel of the ministerial body as they recommend, what has been written here states that any saint that has a TV in their home is inviting themselves towards spiritual regression rather than progression. Some of the antonyms of the word progress are decline, stagnation, and failure. By what this is stating, according to the UPCI manual, any saints who participate in these activities are promoting the hindrance of the body of Christ towards progress and are promoting decline, stagnation, and failure in a spiritual sense.

Granted, it took me quite a bit of time before I finally got TV out of my mind and life. For example, whenever one flies on an airplane, there is, right in front of the person, the capability of watching the movies that are free and available for view. And when I did take the airplane at times or even stayed at a friend's house, there may have been times I viewed movies or programs, gluing my mind to it. Nevertheless, I noticed that there seemed to be an entrancement of some sort while watching it. When the viewing was finished, it was time to get back to reality or real life. Afterwards, it was like waking up to reality: real life seemed different than fictional life, that which makes life pleasant without reality.

And, in returning to Psalm 101:2–8, it clearly points to keeping oneself free from the influence of the world. Today, there is more than meets the eye, one can say, to ridding oneself of TV or movies.

Also, in Germany, when reading the superintendent of the UPCI David Bernard's book entitled *Practical Holiness*, he mentions that the eye is the primary

---

[25] UPCI United Pentecostal Church International Manual 2021 (Missouri: UPCI, 2021), 41.

source by which our thought life is stimulated.[26]Then he further gives Scriptures to substantiate the idea that one should distance himself from the viewing of TV or movies. He also mentions other writers who have also commented about the power of the TV or movies to distract from holy living, being a source of the world to influence to worldly conduct, even violence.

Strict ministers of the UPCI did preach against having a TV. The UPCI, as a body, must have voted for adding the above guidelines into the manual of the UPCI, enough that more agreed than disagreed. Then, it follows that ministers of the UPCI should also teach and preach the same as noted in the Articles of Faith. Today, because it is still in the Articles of Faith, and it has not changed, it still applies. Though, I have been a minister in the UPCI for about twenty years and have been to many UPCI churches from Houston, Texas, to Midland, Michigan, and many churches here and there over the years. To me, it is one of the biggest challenges facing pastors and churches to maintain spirituality and holiness of lifestyle and conduct. The anointed preachers that I have heard that preached against TV very strictly in the pulpit were my spiritual father and the former Kansas District Superintendent Leonard E. Westberg, the strictest preachers I have come across. Scholars and others have written of the content of the TV and the influence of movies on people to commit violent acts.

Younger saints, nevertheless, are faced with a different dilemma surfacing. The Internet is far more entrancing to capture one's lust for a host of websites that will reveal much more than the TV or theaters ever did, all at the click of a mouse and much more privately than the TV. Thus, one today has even more choices for the content one views at home privately, so the battle wages even more seriously, and it is, also, a much more dangerous spiritual warfare.

Yet the Internet has the information available that can be used for much spiritual benefit. Having the Internet is like freedom at one's fingertips: for the good and the bad. With the advent of COVID, suddenly, the eruption of online church services began for the glory of God! It really all depends on the person's usage of the Internet. Therefore, preachers could have mandated that saints in the past rid TV out of their homes, and many probably did, but today, the use of the Internet has made it even more challenging! Today, the Internet's

---

[26] David Bernard, Practical Holiness: A Second Look, Volume 4 (Hazelwood, Missouri: Word Aflame Press, 1985), Loc. 2047 Kindle Version.

usage and content is more private and personal. Because it can be used very beneficially, even used for services to watch in the case of COVID, it appears not to be mandated out of the home. How things have changed so dramatically!

Warning against the influence of the world
Strict preachers outlined the need
To steer clear of such enchanted tubes
With the mindset of Hollywood directors

Influencing the decline of morality
From chewing gum to drugs
One often wonders
How the congregation without warning
Even allows the tube
To find Jezebel in the congregation, too
From the NRA and gun rights of owners
To violent mobs using them for killing
Getting the idea from a tube
Without concern for a soul
Yet the gospel has the power within it
To transform the mind, heart, and soul
To look to Jesus rather than the world
For one's love, entertainment, and fellowship

Yet today, there is the Internet
To click on this or that webpage
Could vary from extremely godly to ungodly
Thus, the need is to get to the heart
Rather than mandate not to use
To instruct in behavioural usage
For the youth
One can imagine
The challenge that is held in one's fingertips

Anointinghood

Thomas Gibson was the first UPCI pastor I had encountered face to face and heard his ministering. In fact, during the time that I had been attending the congregation there in Leesville, LA, only those ministers he invited and he himself did I hear from the UPCI. Even though there had been some evangelists and even some local pastors who had come to preach for the congregation, his preaching (and that of Leonard Westberg) was always the best and the most anointed, I would say! Indeed, his ministering was extremely special, for he had a special knack of preaching under, what would be named as, the anointing.

How can one explain how one preaches with the anointing? And how can one who is a minister preach under the anointing? The former is what the saint hears and views. The latter is the minister having the anointing fall upon himself when he is ministering. There is definitely a need for preachers to preach with the anointing. I have heard some ministers preach under the anointing. In Mexico, it was so common to hear preaching under the anointing. Once preachers received the Holy Spirit during the early 1900s, there must have been several ministers that had something that those who did not receive the Holy Spirit did not possess: the anointing came upon many ministers who had the power of the Holy Spirit. Even so, not all ministers who have the Holy Spirit preach with the anointing. To get the anointing, and this is just my opinion, one must have a special dedication to sacrificing for the kingdom of God in order for God to bless one's ministry when one preaches. I must say that more preachers have the anointing than at any other time in the history of the world.

When one hears it, one picks up the idea that the minister is, in fact, preaching under the anointing. One can say it is a special influence that comes from the throne. It is like the words are fluent, moving speedily through the mouth of the one who God uses, and there seems to be the words provided by God. It is like an extra flame or oil flowing through the mouth of the one who is ministering.

There should be in Bible colleges teaching on preaching with the anointing. There should be a time that the ministerial body of those who minister to ministerial candidates begin seeking for the anointing by asking God for it, for helping other candidates even pray for it, and it be a major concern for the ministerial body.

"Ask, and it shall be given you; seek, and ye shall find; knock, and it shall be opened unto you:[8] for every one that asketh receiveth; and he that seeketh findeth; and to him that knocketh it shall be opened.[9] Or what man is there of you, whom if his son ask bread, will he give him a stone?[10] Or if he ask a fish, will he give him a serpent?[11] If ye then, being evil, know how to give good gifts unto your children, how much more shall your Father which is in heaven give good things to them that ask him?"[27]

Of course, in the gifts of the Spirit, Paul does not mention it. It might have been something later understood and experienced by preachers as they ministered with the power of the Holy Spirit.

Since Jesus taught that it is possible to ask for what one would align with God's will, for the minister, getting the anointing is something that should be sought after. One thing is the calling of God upon one's life; the next thing is getting the anointing. Of course, only God can give the Holy Spirit, and only God can give the anointing upon a preacher, too. The calling that one feels from God is the encouragement from God to pursue one's calling. The diligent study of the word is necessary for the minister, too, but also, with the ministry, there is much potential in getting equipped with gifts from God such as is mentioned in I Corinthians 12, but one of the things that is not mentioned, though, is getting the anointing. That should be, for the one who desires God to provide it to him, to pray for it in diligence and in sacrifice.

The anointing sounds like oil being poured out. For the writers of the New and Old Testament, they were inspired to write the word of God. It was inspiration at its greatest! Yet when one has that same inspiration come for a

---

[27] Matt. 7:7–11

message from God for the church coupled with diligent study and preaching in the pulpit to a group of saints who are apostolic, those who have the power of the Holy Ghost, and speaking the words that God gives, there can be, and should be included with the package, the anointing. To be inspired to write portions of the New and Old Testament is like preaching with the anointing.

What made the difference between how Jesus taught and how the teachers of the Law of Moses taught, according to the people, was that the teachers of the Law of Moses lacked the power that Jesus had when He had taught.

"And came down to Capernaum, a city of Galilee, and taught them on the sabbath days. [32] And they were astonished at his doctrine: for his word was with power.[28]"

The people named it "power," what we name today "the anointing." Usually, though, preachers filled with the Holy Spirit have that possibility to become anointed when they preach. When Thomas Gibson filled the pulpit, he preached under the anointing, because not only was God providing the words to speak, but it was as if there was spiritual oil being poured from heaven upon him as he preached. One might associate speaking in other tongues to preaching in the pulpit. The words a person gets when speaking in tongues is, at the moment, God filling one's mouth with the words to say. Speaking with the anointing is similar: God fills the preacher's mouth not with unintelligible words that nobody understands. Instead, he preaches with words the congregation understands, but God is providing the words to say. Yet it must even go beyond this definition, for many do this; yet they may not be anointed. The anointing is like the Spirit directing rather than the flesh directing. The preacher allows for the Spirit to lead rather than the flesh or himself.

When the anointing came unto the people, the people who received the message distinguished it from others who had preached. They notice an anointing.

The anointing preachers should seek
Enhancing God's message with a special fragrance
To speak with God's direction

---

[28] Luke 4:31–32

Is the pathway to get souls on
When a preacher listens to God
About the message
And studies diligently therein
The word comes nigh

The anointing makes the message clearer
It adds the special tune
Of the word embellished with a red hue
For the congregation to enjoy
The fellowship with the one above
Who anoints

Dutyhood

M y stay in Fort Polk, Louisiana, was a short one of only eleven months. Yet I remember the news coming to me while I was in the field: the commander had come to me personally and had asked about helping my wife get a loan because the company that had sold us the trailer was going to repossess it. I was not shocked but confounded at what had happened. Nevertheless, I agreed to it, then later allowed the company to come and repossess the trailer voluntarily. For only a couple of weeks, my former wife and I, then, had to stay with a church couple that attended the same church, for we were going to leave soon and, really, had no other recourse since I had already received orders for Erlangen, Germany.

For the military, orders were orders, and as a soldier, no one bulked at them. It was a must to travel and live in Germany, but I was thoroughly thankful to God it was not to South Korea since, at that time, soldiers did not bring their spouses with them and duty was for one year. How could a man live without his wife for a year? However, in Germany, married couples had brought their wives, so I was required to contribute that to God's grace, for how can a man being married live alone?

For this duty station, I had to fly alone, though, and stay for a period of time in order to get housing for my former wife and her daughter. Before I was able to find an apartment off base by a German landlord, I had to stay on base in the barracks. In the barracks in Germany, one had his own bed and his own wardrobe. There were probably six guys to a room.

On base, there were announcements for apartments off base and a one-bedroom apartment had come open at the outskirts of the city. The landlord must have been accustomed to having soldiers live in his apartment, for one had just left, and I had seen the advert and responded right away. I scheduled a meeting with the landlord at the apartment and took it without looking at any other apartments or considering any other. Being married, I did not like living alone.

As I recall, the apartment building was about an hour's walk to the Army base, or about a twenty-minute bicycle ride. I had purchased two bikes, one for her and one for me. In Germany, the bikes were different from the Schwinn series. I had bought a Peugeot, which was so much lighter even at that time! I was thrilled! During those days, on Sundays, come to find out, most of the shops, at least in 1986, were closed. There were only small shops located nearby, but there was something I did peek at that had caught my attention! I had noticed their Ritter Sport series of chocolates! Though expensive for me, I had to try them out, and to my surprise, these chocolates were some of the best I had ever tried! When I had a little extra change, I indulged myself on the supreme taste of these chocolates!

When I first arrived, also, I looked for a church to attend. I had no idea if there were UPCI churches in Germany. Yet, I supposed there should have been. Though, I flew over not getting in contact with anyone at home to get me addresses or contact information. I quickly met up with some Christians there who had attended a Baptist congregation. That would do for the short term until I found those of like faith. The pastor of the congregation was an American pastor, I presume, who preached in English to many soldiers or other Americans who made that part of Germany their home.

My duty station was in Erlangen, Germany, a city close to East Germany. When I flew over in January of 1986, Germany was still divided.

Erlangen, Germany, was a part of the former West Germany. I had flown into Frankfurt, Germany, then got transported over to Ferris Barracks in Erlangen, Germany, a city of a population over one hundred thousand. I had arrived in January of 1986, about forty-one years after General George S. Patton had arrived. I had stayed until May of 1987, but the Army base was only active for about another seven years after my departure until June 28, 1994. Ferris was named after Lieutenant Geoffrey Cheney Ferris for a very heroic act.[29]

---

[29] Peter Ferris. "Geoffrey C. Ferris – an American Hero." Leaves from the Ferris Family Tree. Accessed March 12, 2021. http://www.ferrisfamily.us/geoffrey-c-ferris-an-american-hero/.

I had stayed in the barracks for only about two months until Betty and her daughter came over from the USA to join me and move into an apartment off base. During this time, I was diligently attending the congregation that I had been introduced to, but it was only because of necessity and not because of interest in their belief system. In fact, what I had previously experienced, the reception of the Holy Spirit with the evidence of speaking in other tongues, was exactly what the minister had stated that had ceased, possibly with the passing of the apostles. Yet, for me, it happened in my day and even with Betty, who had fallen over backward speaking in other tongues. Further, my experience of dancing at the altar with the commanding presence of God was in no way going to influence me otherwise. Therefore, though faced with a doctrine that seemed to be in opposition to what I had experienced, I felt the need to find a church of like precious faith.

Moreover, it was during these days that I had begun sharing what I had with the other soldiers in the barracks, even to those who went to the church that shared another doctrine. It gave me the opportunity to testify firsthand of what I had experienced to a group of soldiers in the barracks. I was gung-ho about the message I had received back in Leesville, LA. Since I had been living in the barracks, it was also easier to spread the message to the guys living in the barracks, too. My pastor had preached about believing the gospel message as a must, so I brought it to the others in the barracks in a similar way.

Nevertheless, I was in search for a church that shared the same faith as I had.I desired something that held true to the core belief that I had been preached to upon receiving baptism in water in Jesus's name and the reception of the gift of the Holy Spirit with the evidence of speaking in other tongues. On base in Nuremburg, it must have been right after one of the church services that I had been introduced to upon arrival with some of the guys that had attended there, that we went to a café-type restaurant to eat. There, upon chatting with my friends, I happened upon seeing a lady who appeared to be a Pentecostal. Of course, the way Oneness Pentecostals know if someone might be a Oneness Pentecostal is because the ladies do not cut their hair; they wear no makeup or jewelry and wear dresses, at least to their knees (date of observation of this phenomenon: December 1984 to February 1986). In the midst of people coming in and going out, the normal worldly crowd—as I named them—the ladies have their makeup, jewelry, and wear pants, too. However, passing by us was a lady with her husband who had exactly the "uniform" of a Oneness Pentecostal. I was viewing, what one could say, a miracle in action. I was thoroughly interested in striking up a conversation with them.

I excused myself for a minute from my friends to approach the couple and inquire. Upon asking, I had found out that they were, definitely, a Oneness Pentecostal couple, but not only were they Oneness Pentecostals, the couple were UPCI missionaries and the pastoral couple of one of the groups that had met in the chapel on base. God led us to meet right there! Of all the time periods, too, it just so happened that I had approached the other pastor—the one I had listened to for a couple of months at the beginning of my stay in Germany—right before leaving the church and had mentioned of my experience that I had had, to which he expressed his doctrine of disapproval. God was, though, intent on getting me the right congregation at the right time and have me speak to a UPCI missionary named Richard McGriffin on the same day without any of our planning whatsoever! It was all in the plan and hand of God! The missionary's wife was named JoAnn McGriffin. They told me when they had met for services on base with the church congregation, and I was overjoyed that one of the members of their congregation, a Richard Lucas, who had been in Erlangen, Germany, for years, possibly about twenty or so, would be able to pick me up in his car on base in Erlangen for services in Nuremburg! That experience of God working so well within that time frame was a testimony and a miracle in His own way and in His perfect timing, using them to give me the news about where they had congregated, but also that I would have a ride to the services by someone who had been living there for ages! This, obviously, was before all the modern smartphones!

Thus, I give thanks to the Lord that Sister JoAnn McGriffin was faithful to God, especially during those days in dressing as a Oneness Pentecostal. After church service, she did not pluck on makeup, get into jeans, but she continually wore that which Oneness Pentecostals wear. That was the "sign" for me to get into the same church body of my core beliefs.

As of this writing, Richard McGriffin is the superintendent of Hawaii! Beginning this writing, I wished to research exactly where this pastoral couple had ended up in their ministry. I found out that they were still faithful not only to their calling but also to their beliefs even till today! Amen! And God has promoted him to become the superintendent of the work in Hawaii. How God keeps His faithful people doing His work in His way and in His timing!

A miracle in the making
The timing set up by Him
The date, details, and signs given
By the builder of His church

He places people that serve Him
At the right places and at the right times
For fellowship with the right people
To enter into His presence for worship

Extentionhood?

Erlangen, West Germany (so named during that time period), was a small city, but what may have been even smaller yet for us was the one-bedroom apartment we rented. Of course, the rental fees of apartments were higher in comparison to those in Michigan where I had grown up. And this is exactly how the military persuaded those with families to extend their stay overseas: it was to make the situation without extension look almost unbearable. With an extension, however, there were many advantages and benefits that could have been added. I do not want to go into the details, because, in reality, I had no desire to stay in the Army. I had convinced myself to stay in the military only for three years and no longer. Thus, even though it sounded better for the sake of more benefits, I had my eyes set upon a higher calling, to join a much more beneficial military: the officers in God's Army! I declined the offer for extension in Germany, even getting out about three months earlier due to some cuts in military spending. Therefore, my time in Germany was even reduced three months. Thus, after my stay in Erlangen, Germany, for a period of almost a year and a half, in May of 1987, I was on an airplane returning to the USA.

I had received a call of God upon my life, so I was needing, most desperately, to fulfill that call and not extend my time elsewhere not fulfilling the call. Here I must state the need of urgency to fulfill the call of God upon one's life:

Faced with a call from heaven
There are roads to take
One is to immediately find the path
To fulfil that calling
The other is to delay

Yet, another is to ignore

To pastors and ministers who know
Of anyone desiring the ministry
These also can participate in the same paths
For the others who are called
They can immediately assist one to fulfil that heavenly call
Or they can promote a delay for the called
Yet the other is to ignore their calling, too
One must realize that we must give an account
Of how we heeded the call
Were we listening to His voice and command from the beginning?
Or did we delay, even ignore the Master and Judge of souls?

I would say it is a battle
That the enemy would like to win
To delay and stop the one
Who would hear God's calling
For it means less hassle with those
Who help and assist others
To find eternal bliss or be fed from the Master's hand
By means of the called

It could have been, one could say, even a test from God of how much I had valued His calling. Though I had met the missionary to Germany, I did not express my calling, as far as I recall, to him, but I believe he gave me a great recommendation for Texas Bible College, nonetheless. One of the things I wished to do was to get involved somehow in the music ministry, even from the first UPCI church and later in the UPCI church in Nuremburg, but that, unfortunately, never blossomed. To be honest, the music ministry, for me, was like I had given up on it, because I was never encouraged towards that end. I had always felt like I was being buffeted out of that limelight. Of course, I had not played any musical instruments, but I could have, at least I thought I could have, led some songs now and then.

Drivers from America still needed to pass their driver's license in Germany. I did not own a car, and I could not pass the driver's test, either. Twice my ability to pass the written test for a driver's license in Germany did not happen! The missionary was quite upset about it since he had a car for the purpose of bringing people to the chapel for services, but what could I do? His purpose was to provide the missionary car to drive, picking up people to take to the church. However, since I did not and could not pass the driver's exam, he passed the car over to another sister in Bamburg. I guess God did not want me driving on the highways and roads there for some reason. I have driven a car since 1981, a total of, at least, forty years and have been in only one accident that was my fault. In addition, I have only had one speeding ticket. And that is it!

One thing we did start, however, was a Bible study in our small apartment. Yet few ever came. To be honest, I did feel and continue to feel a call of God upon my life, but I had only seen the results to the work of the Lord in Mexico and Kyrgyzstan like I had wished it to be. Yet, for some reason, I concluded of myself quite inadequate to have a large congregation of local followers with a thriving congregation. Nevertheless, I had pastored, later, a congregation of even up to seventy-five persons in Mexico. Notwithstanding, with a congregation of as little as fifteen people, I had really judged myself as not an exceptional pastor.

I was not persuaded with a bribe of more benefits from the Army to extend, though. It was not that I did not enjoy my stay in Germany. I was not intrigued with Army life whatsoever. Further, as I understood later upon learning of the situation in Germany, especially those in a combat MOS of which I was a part of, our time for duty in the field was more than a soldier cared for, probably over two hundred days a year. How could an extension of my military duty help my calling? Surely, the Lord would have been patient with me, but I needed to heed my calling right away and could not wait longer.

Not called to extend for the military
Called to that higher purpose
A duty to study the gospel

A duty to share its precepts
To persuade souls for Jesus
The best calling one could ever have

My Callinghood

In retrospect, let me explain what happened when I had first felt a calling from God in my life, for starters. Back at my first duty station in Fort Polk, LA, and at the first UPCI church with the strictest pastor that I had ever had, my (former) wife and I had moved from the rental home just down the street from the UPCI church to a mobile home we had purchased and had moved into on base at Folk Polk. It was in the mobile home park on base where I had begun feeling the need or the desire for powerful prayer at home and not just at church. During these powerful prayer times, I had felt God impress upon me to enter the ministry. Thus, with those feelings deep within, I had decided that I needed to heed the calling and somehow, some way, enter the ministry. At that time, I had no idea how to begin the calling of God upon my life. Further, I did not discuss it with Pastor Thomas Gibson how I had felt, nor did I really mention it clearly with Missionary McGriffin in Germany, either. I just told him, I believe, that I wanted to attend Bible college. Yet, without saying anything to anybody except my former wife, I began seeking for Bible schools in line with the apostolic doctrine. I had gotten several catalogues from the following UPCI colleges: Texas Bible College, Indiana Bible College, Apostolic Bible College, Christian Life College, and Gateway College of Evangelism. I looked through the materials and had just felt led to Texas Bible College. No offense to the others, but that is what I had felt directed to do. It may have been because I had yearned for the Bible Belt states. It may have been because it was not too long of a drive to my first home church where I had received the Holy Spirit. It may have been because I wanted a distance between my family and my in-laws. And it just may have been the Holy Spirit that had directed me there.

It was during those prayer times as well that I had felt God move upon me in my sleep. I would sometimes wake up in the middle of the night with a powerful presence of God speaking in tongues. It was during the times of the first church in which I had received the Holy Spirit that I was introduced to a church culture with prayer rooms in the church and an encouragement to pray before any and all services, especially before the Sunday night service.

Thus, in weighing my choice of extending my time in Germany, staying in the military about a year and a half longer, without knowing all of the disadvantages of doing so, I was later relieved that I had made my choice not to extend and to come back sooner from overseas duty for another higher calling, the calling of the one who shed His blood for me on Calvary and to preach and teach the gospel message! I was, one could say, eternally thankful for His grace, mercy, and help, so I was set in my mind, after my time of duty, to attend Texas Bible College in Houston, Texas, for the purpose of attending to a higher calling than that of the military. It was a heavenly calling.

During closet hours of prayer
The Master of souls called me
He established a direction
For me to work with Him
I held that calling within my heart
To realize that dream

Setting out to learn
From those who had held
To the same heavenly experience as I
With the most powerful message on earth
For souls to change their paths
From eternal death to eternal life
How could I refuse?

Not only had I gotten Bible college catalogs to choose which to attend after my service in the military, but it was during this time that I began reading in earnest some of the books by David Bernard, who, at that time, was not the superintendent of the UPCI, but his books piqued my interest. His book entitled *Practical Holiness: A Second Look*, with the publishing year of 1985, one year before I came to Germany, and after I ordered the books for a read, I found within the book in chapter twelve entitled "The Sanctity of Human Life."[30] I read that with earnest since I was in the military. For example, he had written, "the killer destroys...the possibility for future salvation in the case of an unsaved person."[31] Reading things like this in his book, I began contemplating that I should not be the cause of an unsaved person losing his life by my use of a rifle. And God must have put these two together, Bernard writing and publishing the book just in time for me to read the book before I was going to the border for border duty between East and West Germany.

Upon entering the military, I had my MOS as a 19D Calvary Scout, and in Germany at that time, it just so happened that our platoon was called for border duty. First, we had to learn what to do in certain circumstances at the border, then we had to present an exam. If we all passed, then we were able to go to the border and perform border duty. Since I had already read about the information concerning the sanctity of human life from Bernard's book, I suppose it was a challenge for me as I was going to answer questions on the exam as to what I would do during certain situations at the border. Thus, though my memory has failed to provide the exact questions on the exam, I do remember, nevertheless, that there were questions regarding using the M16 against the enemy. I answered not according to the answers that they had expected; rather, I answered according to my conscience and according to my belief and agreement with what Bernard had written concerning the sanctity of human life.

After handing in my exam, my platoon sergeant had found out that I had not passed the exam. He was a bit irritated that I had to present the exam again. When he had come to me for a second chance at the exam, I specifically asked him how I should answer, according to the expectations or what I would really do in certain situations, and he said that I should answer according to what I would do rather than what I should do. Therefore, I told him that the answers would remain the same even if I presented the exam again. At that moment, it

---

30 Bernard, *Practical Holiness*. Loc. 4274.
31 Bernard, Loc. 4274.

was like his countenance had changed. He had taken me into his office, and as soon as the door was shut, he took up a ferocious voice like a demon wanting to force me to provide the answers that I was supposed to write as a soldier in the military, shooting to kill if need be. Though he yelled and yelled at me for probably about ten minutes, even another soldier who had brought me to his office was just outside the door must have heard the commotion of grinding teeth. It was the first time I had ever even entered a room with a sergeant to hear him belittle me as such, but I stood firm. I did not budge. I kept to my guns.

Thus, though all the platoon of the Calvary Scouts were heading out for border duty, I got called into the commander's office with a command that I was going to change my MOS. Thus, I was commanded to help the cooks rather than perform border duty for a short period of time. Afterwards, I got moved to ordering parts for the tank battalion on computer. There were requests provided to us to order parts for their platoons in the battalion, so we ordered them by computer, then drove the truck over to pick up the parts. For me, the job was much easier and more relaxing.

Tried by fierce ridicule
By a sergeant probing my thoughts and conscience
Of what I had come to believe
In regard to the sanctity of human life

The trial was put to the test
Within an office to confirm
Whether or not I stood firm
To the belief of not killing another
Who might have been unsaved

Instead, I preferred to use the Bible
To show the unsaved of how to get life
And not being the means by which they may
Lose their life and their chance to eternal life

It was during this time in Germany that my first child was born. We had to take Betty to the military hospital in Nuremburg. She was ready to deliver. One of the benefits that I had experienced with this birth was the fact that I was allowed to remain in the room while, shall I call him, Lester, was born. This was a *normal* birth, I would say, rather than a strange one for the following reasons: First, Lester was born in a hospital rather than at home. Secondly, Betty had had a vaginal birth instead of a C-section. These two items helped me experience watching a baby being born with the hospital staff, doctors, and nurses carrying out their duties of a normal birth.

I had stood to the side and sometimes, obviously, had my view obstructed, because I was not really at the end but more to the side and just trying to keep Betty calm, in a sense, that I was there. Yet if I were to put myself in her shoes, I would think that having a child at a hospital would have been, for me, embarrassing. First, the birth mother is the centre of attention at that moment, but all of the attention is also centred around the vagina, where the child will come out. Secondly, the one area that is overwhelmingly private is made the center of attention for a number of staff at the hospital simply for the birth of a baby.

The most embarrassing thing about having a child born in the hospital is the fact that the man whose wife is having a baby, all these strange people, foreign to him, are trying to care for the delivery of the child, but they also have access to seeing the baby come forth and be delivered.

Yet the child was delivered without incident, really, or any extra time or effort needed from the staff at the hospital to administer any extra care and attention.

Having a child may be embarrassing
For the mother and dad both
The baby comes out of the most private section
And makes its debut at an entry and exit point
That is not permissible for view by others
Except only just mom and dad

Except in this occasion

Of the gathering crew
Expecting a view
Of the baby that is new
But on this occasion
Baby finds both mom and dad
Strangely with a deep red hue
In their faces, wondering
Is this common for moms and dads
To have such a red hue?

The dad could answer back
It was all for a place
That had not been permittable to view
But only between the two
So widely visible in that heated moment
That little baby came through

Returnhood

To leave military duty was for me a blessing, knowing that I could no longer be the cause of someone who might be unsaved to lose their life. Thus, in retrospect, it was confirmed to me by those circumstances not to extend. The days that I returned home was deeply remembered. My former wife had left earlier than I and arrived home. I had to fly to another city to process out of the military, and that flight was deeply remembered. I was going to prepare for entrance to the service of the King! It was one of the best feelings of my life, not only leaving the military but also on route to prepare for the best service, to spread the message of the gospel!

Why would God choose me to enter the ministry? Why would He want me to deliver the message of the gospel to others? I could only fathom or think that He might be mistaken as others may have thought, but to the contrary, He was not mistaken in any way!

This brings me to a thought regarding ministers who are either assisting other younger ministers to get on the road to assist others, too, or to be a roadblock for success for others. To me, the calling of God, the ministry, is not just a pastoral gig. It is, in light of Ephesians, a work of many in order to help others perceive and receive the whole gospel, the whole word of God, for their perfection.

Thus, some may try and thwart a person's calling. When a person has a calling, and since God does the calling, it is of the utmost importance to assist others, too, in their calling. To assist others in their calling is not just at Bible school, but it is, or should be, at every church, especially in our case, since we hold the truth, evident that we should be those who try to make it possible that others are involved and that we get involved, too, in helping others.

"And he gave some, apostles; and some, prophets; and some, evangelists; and some, pastors and teachers;[12] For the perfecting of the saints,

for the work of the ministry, for the edifying of the body of Christ:[13] Till we all come in the unity of the faith, and of the knowledge of the Son of God, unto a perfect man, unto the measure of the stature of the fulness of Christ:[14] That we *henceforth* be no more children, tossed to and fro, and carried about with every wind of doctrine, by the sleight of men, *and* cunning craftiness, whereby they lie in wait to deceive;[15] But speaking the truth in love, may grow up into him in all things, which is the head, *even* Christ."[32]

---

[32] Eph. 4:11–15

Triphood

Since I had been accepted at Texas Bible College, which was, for me, a means to get prepared for ministry, the timing was quite perfect. I had processed out of the military in May of 1987, and I had been accepted for the fall term of 1987, which would commence the beginning of September. Thus, I had a short period of time to be with family again and set out on the new adventure of attending Bible college. Before the adventure for Bible college began, and still while in Germany, my former wife, as named by me in this writing as Betty and had already had Carol as her daughter, we also had our first child together, whom I shall name just for this writing *Lester*. Therefore, we had the responsibility of two children by that time, her first daughter and our first child, Lester.

By then, all of us were in Midland, Michigan, again visiting with family and getting ready to prepare for the trip to Houston, Texas, as Texas Bible College was there located at that time. The thought might come to one, how can you just get up and go to Bible college not having prepared any apartment or housing in Houston before journeying out into the unknown and not even having a job there yet? In those days, even without modern smartphones, there was faith in the fact that God would provide for us.

Further, the Honda Civic was no longer with us. It passed away. However, from the in-laws, who were gracious enough to provide another car of theirs that they wanted to give to us, an Oldsmobile Cutlass with a six-cylinder engine (I would not have remembered that since I was never the mechanic type nor interested in cars, but since we suffered along the way down to Texas, it will not be forgotten).

I assume Oldsmobile is a great car. We just had a horror story unfold on the way down to Texas that, for us, was almost unbearable, but we lived through it, through the pain of not being able to get there quickly. What was the problem? Since Betty, Carol, Lester, and I had just come from Germany, we had not much to our name. The first time we had traveled down to Louisiana, we had to get a U-Haul truck because we had more belongings. After having moved overseas and having to pay for our own shipping expenses, we tossed those unnecessary things and just made do with essentials. Thus, for our trip down to Houston, we only needed a U-Haul trailer that would be attached to the back of our Oldsmobile. That was what gave us a headache all the way to Houston.

You see, the six-cylinder, unbeknownst to us at the time of preparation, did not have enough power to haul the U-Haul trailer with all our belongings in it. Or, one could say, it did have the power, but it overheated often. I was not, then, probably not even now, aware of the capacity to know that one should check everything well before departure if it will be convenient for us. However, even if one would have tried it out, that part of having the car overheat would never have been found out in any case. Why not? Well, first of all, it did not start its first overheating, I believe, until we got down to about the area of Chicago or so. And, back then, we did not have cell phones. In other words, from around the Chicago area and on down to Houston, Texas, a distance of over one thousand miles, and though, as I understand from research, the speed limit had increased to sixty by that year in some areas, from Chicago and on, I could not drive but thirty to thirty-five miles per hour due to the car overheating.

I had brought some coolant in the trunk of the car and had a sufficient supply of it. It was, as to my recollection, about every thirty miles or so we had to stop due to the car overheating. Along the highway, with two kids in the backseat of the car, with the heat getting hotter, and not knowing if putting on the air conditioner at that time would affect driving performance too, I kept the air conditioner off. Thus, the trip turned out to be a long-lasting journey. I was visited by a police officer, as I recall, once, and not really to help but just to state that I should not be parked on a bridge. He stated that I should move my car off of it (while the car was overheated). Nevertheless, through all the hardships of stopping and waiting for the car to cool down, of using more coolant to put into the radiator, we finally were able to get to our destination. Yet, one could say, we might have been exhausted and ready for a home; the task of finding one began upon arrival, besides my need of finding work.

Through all of that, I never once considered, and neither did Betty, of turning around and heading home again. We had already mapped out our plans. Moreover, we had already gone too far for even thinking about it. In addition, we never once had thought about renting a car. Of course, I have no recollection of knowing how much we had saved for the trip and for the expenses of finding an apartment or a house, but that might have been one of the reasons why I sought no help, for the costs might have been too much. Thus, we suffered stopping every thirty miles for a trip of one thousand miles for a period of possibly twenty minutes, at least, each stop. In view of this, we possibly stopped about thirty-three times, and if we had stopped for twenty minutes each stop, we were on the side of the highway waiting for the car to cool down for a time period in total of somewhere around eleven hours for the entire trip! Those eleven hours included just waiting on the side of the road for the car to cool down! For the sake of travel, I believe that that trip was one of, if not the worst trip on the road I have ever had! I was not angry at Oldsmobile, nor U-Haul, nor called either one to tell them of the problem, either. We grinned and bore the entire journey with two kids in the car probably wondering what was really happening with their lives! A nightmare would not describe this; it was worse than that! A nightmare lasts a short time at night; this lasted about eleven hours!

Who could I blame for this? I could blame no one, not the car manufacturer, not God, not the devil, not U-Haul, not my parents, not the Bible college, not a minister, not a saint, not my former wife, not the children, not the contents that we were carrying either; it just happened by chance, I suppose that no one might have expected this to happen! But it did, and it happened before I was to be involved in learning at Bible college preparing for the ministry. Maybe, one could say, that was God's way of humbling us.

Thirty-five miles an hour I could only drive
On a trip of one thousand miles
Eleven hours of waiting off the road

On a trip that was worse than a nightmare
However, God was with us each step
The car-maintained course
Because the angels were watching
And they helped the car do its job
To get us there without losing the engine
Nor us losing our minds!

Houstonhood

We were so relieved upon arriving in Houston! We sought refuge at a hotel until we got tidied up and rested up from our journey. Then, I headed off to the college to make inquiry and asked for any job openings or apartments available. Finding an apartment was not difficult, for one was found quite easily; yet it might not have been the best type of apartment. Yet I was in no mood to argue, and possibly neither was my former wife at that time. Instead, finding a place we could call home throughout all that ordeal and start with my plans of attending Bible college, even finding work, was all in the making and on the calendar that God had prepared.

The area of which the Bible college was located was just inside the Southeast loop. It was just within that area, not too far from the college, also, we had found an apartment. The city itself was quite fast-paced. To get from one part of the city to the other, one had to take the highway. And I was on a quest to find work. It was not too long afterwards I had found a job at a place called Sundown Auto Storage. This was a storage lot for cars that had been towed, either because they had parked illegally, or they had been in an accident and were undriveable. I was able to get work there for the second shift as an office clerk full time.

This job offered the opportunity for me to get homework done from the Bible college during the time I was at work. At work, also, if any tow trucks had come in with cars, I had to check them in by noting the contents, car model, year, and, overall, the information about the car's condition. If anyone had come to pick up their cars, they would have to make payment in cash only and no change was given. It was my job to figure out the cost for them to pick up their car, take the money, and allow them to take their car once the storage fees and the towing fees were paid in full. At times, I also used a forklift to move the cars around in the lot. This job sustained me while I was at Bible college, and it also helped provide for the family.

I studied for three years at the Bible college. The teachers at the college had provided their own materials. The most well-versed teacher was Kelsey Griffin. He brought forward great material for the students.

At the college, there was the opportunity provided that some of the Bible school students were afforded the opportunity to preach in the local churches. There were three, perhaps four, of the students that would go to a local church that offered the opportunity. We were scheduled to preach in the service at different times, even give forth Sunday school lessons. One Sunday, I went with a group of these Bible college students to a local church. It would be the first time that I would preach. I had grown up in church as a young lad and, at that time, had studied to some degree of Bible college, but I had never been offered the opportunity to give Sunday school or preach a message to the congregation. The only opportunity I remember was in Germany. I had taught the Bible at home for a cell group, which consisted only of my family and Mr. Lucas, who had picked us up for church on Sundays. Thus, for me to have this opportunity of preaching that Sunday was a blessing, but I was also quite nervous to say the least.

Yet, I still remember the topic of the sermon that I had preached for the first time. It was about the Good Samaritan. It was only about ten minutes long, yet I tried my best to apply it to today; how do we help those desperately in need?

One day, some of the Bible school students wanted to have an all-night prayer meeting. Some were all for it; I was one of those willing. The day came, and we started the prayer. For us, the way we pray is by having us pray any way we wish: walking, sitting, standing, kneeling, etc. On that night, I was very pleased to be at prayer, but I noticed that after a few hours some of the other students began leaving. I had thought they had wanted to stay for the entire night. Yet, for some reason—I think it was the cornbread I ate—I had begun passing some gas. It was not loud coming out at all, but it did come out silently, and as long as I was praying, it kept on coming! For me, I could not hold the gas at all. It was just not possible. Albeit, I hoped that their leaving was not due to the problem of my passing gas that night.

Then came another day when Betty was ready for delivery of my second child, her fourth. With that discovery and the fact that I was no longer in the service, the hospital expenses, which I needed to take on and would have been overwhelming for a college student and with the added member of the family, totaling five already, very expensive. I had decided, and Betty agreed to the plan, of having a midwife that would deliver the child in the home. All was set and ready. The instruction that she had needed to attend, she did. Nothing seemed extraordinary. The time came for the baby to be delivered; however, and it was found that, the baby was not in the proper position for best delivery. Its head was not at the opening of the vagina. The midwife decided, then, it best to have the child in the hospital instead of having it home delivery. Though we had already paid all the fees for the home delivery, we had no say whatsoever or control whatsoever in what the midwife would do. She refused to perform the delivery at our home, so we had no other choice but to go ahead and have the child delivered at the hospital. With all my research and under-standing of having home delivery, it was the best choice, especially concerning the costs. Yet with that refusal of hers, that just meant that I would have to pay, what might just be, the most expensive birth plan, midwife payment and hospital expenses dues for a birth. However, because the baby's head was not at the opening of the vagina, that just meant, also, that the doctor would pre-scribe to have the baby delivered C-section instead. That trip to the hospital was a horror story for me in regard to finances. Of course, the birth of the baby boy would bring us great joy, but with having to foot a bill that was so expensive with my employment, it would seem unreal, to say the least.

Jake, as I shall call my second boy, was delivered by C-section without my consent and without my wishes as to the way he was delivered. However, even though I was not content with the way he had come out, I would still be pleased that God had provided for us another son. It just meant, though, that I would have to pay the entire bill without any regard to the choice of how the child was born. I was quite angry, bitter, and happy all at the same time. Yet I could do nothing, and I saw nothing in the hospital, for I could not be in the delivery room that time.

Forced to have no choice in the matter
My second son was born
It may even have been dramatic for all
The mother having a birth without seeing her son
A father wondering whether the child was okay
It was a cold process with no warmth to speak of
But seeing him and holding him
Really put away all those troubles
Like a mother undergoing stress and pain
During the delivery
All is forgotten once the child is in her arms
Happiness, then, ensues

At the end of the three years at the Bible college, which I had hoped would extend into four, but it did not, my former wife and I had returned back to Midland, Michigan, in hopes to get involved in the church work there. To have moved so many times in the past was a bit weary, one might say, but it offered the opportunity for a person to get loads of experience. For example, I had gotten experience not only from the Bible college, but also, on Sundays, we attended a local church, and that church, by mandate from the Bible college, had to be changed every six months. We would not only be observers, but we would try to get involved in the work one way or another.

Midlandhood

We returned to Midland to look for opportunities in ministry. I did write my first pastor in the UPCI, but the area there might have been incredibly challenging to find work to support the family. Even returning to Midland might have been quite difficult to find work. That became one of the problems on that return journey.

The first challenge was the rift that formed between the local pastor and I because of what I had preached. I will name the pastor, Pastor Alfred. Pastor Alfred was a jolly fellow, and he seemed really nice. He even provided the opportunity one day to preach a short fifteen-minute sermon after the Sunday school when all the rest of the people had returned to the sanctuary for the short message. Thus, the adults had received their Sunday school lesson and the kids did, too, but they had gone into their different classrooms.

At their return, I was signaled to preach for the first time in that congregation. Of course, again, I was so nervous. I do not believe that I had ever preached more than once at Bible college, and this was the second time. The first message I preached was about the Good Samaritan, and the second was this one. Upon getting into the pulpit and preaching, I had mentioned about holiness issues. I did counsel with him beforehand, and he had mentioned to let God's Spirit do the leading. Although, I did notice that he felt quite hesitant at the way he said it. After the preaching, the pastor had thought that I should not have brought up any of those things up that I did bring up. Thus, though I had mentioned certain things about dress and jewelry and maybe even TV, the pastor had disagreed with my message. Thus, he had felt that I overstepped my boundary in what he thought was only the pastor's responsibility, of preaching on holiness.

Later, he had strictly mentioned to me in a private conversation that I was not to do that again. Once he delivered that news, I thought it best if my family just start another church and be separate from that congregation. Thus, my family and I had invited my other family members and some people from the neighborhood to come to our congregation at the home. As per a job, I did not have one, but starting out ministering as such and having some people come and listen to the word of God, that was enough for us to sustain us for the time being. I considered not looking for part-time work; instead, I only dedicated my time to the gospel and in ministering to those who had come to our services.

What had happened was even brought to the attention of Texas Bible College, too. In fact, the president's son called me on the phone and had given me some advice. He had mentioned that I should return to the church and apologize to the pastor. In my mind, I was only doing that which I should have done, and that is preach the word and preach what some in the movement had believed, and that was holiness. I could not comprehend why I should apologize for trying to stick with the message that I believe that God had given to me. The only thing that I had done was just leave and not say anything to him directly of that. That, I suppose, was getting me into trouble.

Yet, I was stubborn and did not believe that I had done anything wrong. To the contrary, I thought that I had listened to God, had provided the right message, and was simply following His orders. But there were the orders of the pastor that was saying the opposite of that. Who was I to follow, then? Was I to buckle and give in?

With some family members and other people attending the small congregation I had at our home, and the fact that I saw nothing wrong with trying to express my biblical understanding of Scripture in the church, I decided just to hold on to what I had done and not apologize, per se, to the pastor for sticking to what I had preached.

What had transpired next was the third baby that we were to have together was ready to be born. As previously in Houston, Texas, we had contacted and met with a midwife for the purpose of having the child at home instead of in the hospital due to the rising costs of childbirth.

On December 25th, Christmas Day, the child was ready to be born. We had called the main midwife, but she was, again, not willing to come to our home to conduct this birth. This time, it was not a matter of the position of the child, so I was determined, and a bit distraught, too, of this conduct from the midwifery. Yet, even if they decided not to come, I was going to have the baby born at home with or without them. It got to the stage that the baby was ready to come out. We had called the assistant midwife and told her that we were going to have the birth done at home and if she would just come and observe that nothing went wrong and help with a few things, that would be awesome. She finally relented and offered to be at our place. Thus, I was able to firsthand watch our third child be born and actually hold the baby first when it came out. The chord was cut; the baby was a fine-looking baby girl. Thus, we had a family of six already.

Then, my parents decided on not coming back to the services we conducted at our home due to their belief system as different. There was a rift between my belief system and theirs, but in a different area. That is, with what I had come to believe was the Oneness of God, and what my parents had believed was in the Trinity Doctrine. And though I tried to convince them in preaching, they still held firm to what they had believed, too.

Thus, with the congregation dwindling and the funds dwindling, I had to find something else, add to, or find somewhere else to go. It was about that time, then, that we actually returned to the former church in which the problem had started. Thus, in reality, we had no funds coming in, so I began selling some of our stuff in a sale in order to get by. Though I do not think I apologized either to the pastor, as I thought the same, I was just coming back to attend.

And that is where some of the other problems began surfacing.

First of all, I needed to find work, yet during that period of time, it was very difficult to find work. Secondly, we had actually left Midland for a short period of time and went all the way to Kansas. There, we did not find exactly what we needed, so we returned to Midland. It was in this return that we no longer had the apartment and had to live with my former wife's parents for the time being. That said, in trying to run the affairs of our home at the in-law's house only caused more trouble. Of course, they believed not the way we did; further, I was not in favor of the kids watching TV, either. And, they had one, and that is what they would watch as soon as it was turned on.

With the strictness, one could say, that I had held onto, even trying to get the family members to cooperate, the in-laws basically had had enough of it. Finally, Dad-in-law had said I needed to leave.

Abuse, said they
Thus, I had to go
Nowhere to turn
Just my parents' place to sojourn

I had kept order
For their benefit
Yet, the accusation came
To me from the enemy
Due to keeping them from
Disobedience

It seemed that no one liked
The strictness to which
A parent had kept
The four children
In line, you see.

An accusation stemmed
From the advisory board, you see
That mandated separation of child and parent
That mandate came not from government
It came from the in-laws and an unexpected source
A pastor who thought it best to separate
The ones that God had united

To me, the verse said the man was obligated to correct his son, and in so doing, as it says, *with the rod*, that would be the means by which the son would be delivered!

"Withhold not correction from the child: for *if* thou beatest him with the rod, he shall not die. [14] Thou shalt beat him with the rod, and shalt deliver his soul from hell.[33]"

---

[33] Prov. 23:13

Here is a promise. In Deuteronomy 6, God had spoken to Moses about telling the people that they should teach their children the concepts that he had taught them. King Solomon, the one who had written most of Proverbs, was a wise king in that God had given him wisdom, and that wisdom, no doubt, was from God. The wisdom that he speaks of here, giving us a verse of scripture that has a promise to it, is to beat children with the rod to deliver them. No one knows but God the judgment that a person will have upon his life at the end. However, the promise through the word of God for the people of God is to beat their children to deliver their souls as they grow up and get old. In the end, at the judgment seat, their souls would be delivered from hell! It refers to eternal death, that which the Christian wants to be delivered from!

In view of this scripture and others, since I had studied these, I was of the viewpoint that I was required to do such to deliver my children from hell. Thus, I was not going to listen to anyone that would counsel otherwise, because, simply put, no one can change the promise of God. In fact, the one that would want to change this idea in the minds of people would be, no doubt, the enemy, because he is after their soul.

Studied the scripture here at this verse
There was no getting around it
By compromise to suit the will of man
The will of God was clearly written
For there was a promise and a responsibility

For those who were called of God
It was not my word but His to obey
In order for eternal life to be had
By my descendants
Which would you choose?

My deep profound desire
Was for them to hold onto life

To enter heaven where the saved long to go
And not end up on a dead-end road

Because of the separation placed upon me, I had to return to my parents'
home, of course, without any of the other family members with me, for they
were, one could say, captured in the other home. I am not sure where my former
wife stood with all of it, and why the question did not come up of, "Why not
come to my parent's home, then?" It did not surface, because, inwardly, I reckon
she felt the same as they had. I must have been booted out of the home so that
they could live their lives in peace without me.

Albeit, one thing more was a problem. The pastor of the church, his wife,
my former wife, and I had had a conversation. My former wife had started
bringing up the affairs of the home and how strict I was, relating this news to
the pastor with some intention. I guess she wished to curb my strictness
through the pastor. No doubt, the pastor may have felt a little bitter of what
had transpired earlier on. And he was dead set against how strict I held onto
my belief system in the administration of it in my home or with my family,
shall I say. Thus, it appears that just in hearing my former wife mention the
problems that were transpiring with me and my strictness, he made a judgment, per se. The judgment he made was that my former wife and I should
separate. In fact, he mentioned the word separate after hearing my former
wife's speech of things that were happening. Nevertheless, and what was a bit
irritating to me was, the pastor had not listened to my side of the story at all.
In fact, what really surprised me was that he was making all his decisions only
based on what she was bringing forth and not hearing anything that I had to
say. One could say it this way: because I was too strict, I was being ostracized
from my own family. The pastor recommended or commanded, not sure
which, that we separate. Upon hearing what he had determined that we should
or must do without taking into consideration anything that I might say in rebuttal, I just left the conversation without saying anything to anyone.

What was it that turned against me?

Was it my own family?
The in-laws were expected to side with the former wife
But she took it further
And brought it before the pastor
And the pastor unfortunately made
A decision without full counsel
In his opinion he stated
That my former wife and I should separate

I was in a state of shock
Relieved of my duties
One could say, both from the in-laws
And the pastor who sided against me

I was to change by their mandate
Of not being so strict
On the congregation and the family
Without any rebuttal from me
For my testimony did not matter
Nor the fact that I should have been the head
Of my own family
Maybe I was too strict
Yet, that gives no reason
To separate a man from his family
In fact, the one who should make the decisions
Should not it be the one who God approved
To have that authority in the home?

Returned to my parents' home
In the state of shock
With a red face
Trying to explain
How I had been ostracized
For being too strict

For them, they, too, would not agree
With my strictness, per se
Yet they would not agree
With the separation of a family
Thus, the only resolve I had
Was to get my family away
From the influence of the in-laws
And to a place where I could be recognized
As the head of my own family

In retrospect, I do agree I was quite strict with my own family, but that does not give anyone the right to stop a person from the right of having a family.

Having the following scripture in my mind and comparing it to what the pastor said, I was like…huh?

"Wherefore they are no more twain, but one flesh. What therefore God hath joined together, let not man put asunder."[36]

Since I was young, I was not into the argumentative mode with any pastor, so I would not have given a rebuttal. To me, instead of giving a rebuttal, my rebuttal was expressed in my quick leaving from the scene.

Thus, I returned to my parents' home without any children; we had three together by that time, and she had had her daughter, too, so that made four total, but I seemed not to be a part of it anymore.

So, I was contemplating what I needed to do, for all did not look well regarding the relationship at church, to the relationship with the in-laws, with the family at the in-laws, and with no job and no prospect of a job that would sustain a family of six in the city of Midland during those years.

In my mind, I did have a solution. The solution, to me, was to leave Midland, get away from the in-laws so that I could run the family as I should or the way I would. Therefore, I was looking for work outside of Midland, outside of town, and something remarkably interesting had crossed my path: there was an announcement for a job in Mexico to teach English.

Bibliography

"Abortion." Merriam-Webster. Accessed March 10, 2021. http://www.merriam-webster.com/dictionary/abortion.

Bernard, David. *Practical Holiness: A Second Look, Volume 4.* Hazelwood, Missouri: Word Aflame Press, 1985.Kindle Version.

Bhandari, Smitha."Causes of Mental Illness." WebMD.June 30, 2020.http://www.webmd.com/mental-health/mental-health-causes-mental-illness.

Farlex. "Words containing hood." The Free Dictionary. Accessed March 10, 2021. http://www.thefreedictionary.com/words-containing-hood.

Ferris, Peter. "Geoffrey C. Ferris – an American Hero." Leaves From the Ferris Family Tree. Accessed March 12, 2021. http://www.ferrisfamily.us/geoffrey-c-ferris-an-american-hero/.

"Historical Background and Development of Social Security." *Social Security History*. Accessed June 19th, 2021. https://www.ssa.gov/history/briefhistory3.html.

"Insane." Dictionary.com. Accessed March 11, 2021. https://www.dictionary.com/browse/insane.

Kling, Jim. "Mad Cow Disease Restricts Blood Donation." WebMD. February 21, 2003. http://www.webmd.com/men/news/20030221/mad-cow-scare-linked-to-blood-shortage.

Malkmus, George Rev. "NEW BOOK! God's Original Diet – By Rev. George Malkmus." Hallelujah Diet. Accessed March 11, 2021. https://www.myhdiet.com/healthnews/rev-malkmus/new-book-gods-original-diet-by-rev-george-malkmus/.

Romig, Kathleen. "Social Security Lifts More Americans Above Poverty Than Any Other Program." Center on Budget and Policy Priorities.

Accessed March 11, 2021.https://www.cbpp.org/research/social-security/social-security-lifts-more-americans-above-poverty-than-any-other-program.

Smith, Michael David. "Gallup Poll Shows Football Overwhelmingly Americans' Favorite Sport." NBCSports. January 10, 2018. https://profootballtalk.nbcsports.com/2018/01/10/gallup-poll-shows-football-overwhelmingly-americans-favorite-sport/.

Stevens, Chris. "Jozwiak Still Involved with the Game He Loves." Midland Daily News. March 24, 2016. https://www.ourmidland.com/news/article/Jozwiak-still-involved-with-the-game-he-loves-7024892.php.

Taylor, Derrick Bryson. "Two Milwaukee Children Shot After Throwing Snowballs at Cars, Police Say (Published 2020)." The New York Times. January 7, 2020. http://www.nytimes.com/2020/01/07/us/milwaukee-snowball-shooting.html.

UPCI United Pentecostal Church International Manual 2021. Missouri: UPCI, 2021.

"Why Midland." City of Midland. Accessed June 4th, 2022. https://cityofmidlandmi.gov/1828/Why-Midland.